Correspondences, Interviews and Conversations with Sri Aurobindo and The Mother

Compiled by Avadhani
(Bhanabhai G. Patel)

Published by Avadhani (Bhanabhai G. Patel)
28 Westminster Gardens, Barkingside, Ilford,
Essex IG6 1PL, UK

Publisher:
Avadhani
(Bhanabhai G. Patel)
28 Westminster Gardens
Barkingside, Ilford
Essex IG6 1PL, UK

ISBN 0-9545855-0-X

First Edition 15th August 2002
Price £2.00   U.S.A. $3.00
in India Rs. 90.00

Printer:
The Maypole Press Ltd.
The Acorn Centre, Roebuck Road
Hainault, Ilford,
Essex IG6 3TU

Avadhani – the spiritual name given by the Mother to Bhanabai G. Patel on 6th June 1954. Avadhani meaning careful.

Compiler's Note

Who knows Sri Aurobindo and the Mother?
Nobody.

I had an interview with the Mother in 1954 and collected some more interviews with Sri Aurobindo and the Mother. I then compiled some conversations and correspondences which throws some light on their Personalities and gives glimpses of their Truth Consciousness.

Avadhani
(Bhanabhai G. Patel)

CONTENTS

SECTION I

SECTION II

SECTION III

Conversations

SECTION IV

Appendixes

SECTION I

Talk of 7 April 1929

Will you say something to us about Yoga?

WHAT do you want the Yoga for? To get power? To attain to peace and calm? To serve humanity?

None of these motives is sufficient to show that you are meant for the Path.

The question you are to answer is this: Do you want the Yoga for the sake of the Divine? Is the Divine the supreme fact of your life, so much so that it is simply impossible for you to do without it? Do you feel that your very *raison d'être* is the Divine and without it there is no meaning in your existence? If so, then only can it be said that you have a call for the Path.

This is the first thing necessary—aspiration for the Divine.

The next thing you have to do is to tend it, to keep it always alert and awake and living. And for that what is required is concentration—concentration upon the Divine with a view to an integral and absolute consecration to its Will and Purpose.

Concentrate in the heart. Enter into it; go within and deep and far, as far as you can. Gather all the strings of your consciousness that are spread abroad, roll them up and take a plunge and sink down.

A fire is burning there, in the deep quietude of the heart. It is the divinity in you—your true being. Hear its voice, follow its dictates.

There are other centres of concentration, for example, one above the crown and another between the eye-brows. Each has its own efficacy and will give you a particular result. But the central being lies in the heart and from the heart proceed all central movements—all dynamism and urge for transformation and power of realisation.

What is one to do to prepare oneself for the Yoga?

To be conscious, first of all. We are conscious of only an insignificant portion of our being; for the most part we are unconscious. It is this unconsciousness that keeps us down to our unregenerate nature and prevents change and transformation in it. It is through unconsciousness that the undivine forces enter into us and make us their slaves. You are to be conscious of yourself, you must awake to your nature and movements, you must know why and how you do things or feel or think them; you must understand your motives and impulses, the forces, hidden and apparent, that move you; in fact, you must, as it were, take to pieces the entire machinery of your being. Once you are conscious, it means that you can distinguish and sift things, you can see which are the forces that pull you down and which help you on. And when you know the right from the wrong, the true from the false, the divine from the undivine, you are to act strictly up to your knowledge; that is to say, resolutely reject one and accept the other. The duality will present itself at every step and at every step you will have to make your choice. You will have to be patient and persistent and vigilant—"sleepless", as the adepts say; you must always refuse to give any chance whatever to the undivine against the divine.

Is the Yoga for the sake of humanity?

No, it is for the sake of Divinity. It is not the welfare of humanity that we seek but the manifestation of the Divine. We are here to work out the Divine Will, more truly, to be worked upon by the Divine Will so that we may be its instruments for the progressive incorporation of the Supreme and the establishment of His reign upon earth. Only that portion of humanity which will respond to the Divine Call shall receive its Grace.

Whether humanity as a whole will be benefited, if not directly, at least, in an indirect way, will depend upon the condition of humanity itself. If one is to judge from the present conditions, there is not much hope. What is the attitude today of the average man—the representative humanity? Does he not rise in anger and revolt directly he meets something that partakes of the genuinely divine? Does he not feel that the Divine means the destruction of his cherished possessions? Is he not continually yelling out the most categorical negative to everything that the Divine intends and wills? Humanity will have to change much before it can hope to gain anything by the advent of the Divine.

How is it that we have met?

We have all met in previous lives. Otherwise we would not have come together in this life. We are of one family and have worked through ages for the victory of the Divine and its manifestation upon earth.

The Mother
"Bulletin of Sri Aurobindo International Centre of Education"

9

In 1970, in the first days of Auroville's pioneering community experiment of Aspiration, a group of its members went to The Mother once a week for guidance on their myriad communal difficulties. In this first talk, The Mother was asked about the right attitude in work.

THE MOTHER

Talks With Aspiration

Each man has his own solution and that is the great difficulty, yet we must find a way for all the solutions to work together.

(silence)

The framework must be vast, very supple and we must have a lot of good will. This is the first condition, an individual condition: a good will to be supple enough to do at each moment the best thing to be done.

...there is a long way to go between what we are and what we must be; and for that we must be very supple, we must never lose sight of the goal, but know that we cannot jump to it in a single bound but must find the means. That is much more difficult, even more difficult than to make the inner discovery. In fact, the inner discovery should be made before coming here.

For there is a starting point: when you have found in yourself the light that doesn't flicker, the presence which can guide you with certainty, when you become aware that constantly, at every moment, there is an opportunity to learn something and that, in the present state of matter, there is always a progress to be made.

That is how one should arrive, anxious to discover the progress to be made at each moment. You see, to have a life which wants to grow and perfect itself, that must be the collective ideal of Auroville: "a life that wants to grow and perfect itself" – not in the same manner for everyone, not at all, each one in his own way. So, there are thirty of you, it's difficult, isn't it? When there will be thirty thousand of you, it'll be easier because, naturally, there will be many more possibilities. You are the pioneers, you have the most difficult task, but I feel it is the most interesting one, because you must establish in a concrete, durable and evolving way the attitude required to be truly an Aurovilian, to learn daily the lesson of the day. Each sunrise brings an opportunity for discovery. So, in this spirit we discover, each one discovers.

And the body needs activity. If you 'keep it inactive, it will begin to revolt through illness, etc. It needs really material activity, like planting flowers, building a house. One must feel what is needed. There will be those who do exercise, those who go bicycling; there are innumerable possible activities. But in your little group you must come to an agreement so that each individual can find the activity which best suits his temperament, his nature and his needs. But not with ideas, ideas are not much good. Ideas give you prejudices, such as "that is a good work" or "this work is not worthy of me" and all that sort of nonsense. There is no bad work. There are bad workers, but there is no bad work. All work is good when done in a good way. And it is a kind of communion; therefore, if you are so fortunate as to be conscious of an inner light, you will see that through your manual work you call the Divine down into things. Then the communion becomes very concrete, there is a whole world to be discovered, and it is marvelous.

You are young, you have all the time before you. And to be young, to be really young, it is necessary always, always to keep growing, always to develop yourselves, always to progress. Growth is the sign of youth, and to grow in consciousness, you know, is unlimited. I know old people of twenty and young folk of fifty, sixty, seventy years. And if we do manual work, we keep ourselves in good health. So now, it is up to you to find the solution.

All that you can do...There are all sorts of things...All sorts...So then, among yourselves see what you can do, see how it can come out. Then you will come to tell me. All right?

10 March 1970

'SRI AUROBINDO ACTION'
January 1975

I am charged by God
　　　to do his mighty work,
Uncaring I serve his will
　　　who sent me forth,
Reckless of peril and
　　　earthly consequence.
I reason not of virtue
　　　and of sin
But do the deed he has put
　　　into my heart.

(Savitri)   – Sri Aurobindo

The Mother on Savitri

(a report written from memory)

Do you read Savitri?

Yes, Mother, yes.

You have read the whole poem ?

Yes, Mother, I have read it twice.

Have you understood all that you have read ?

Not much, but I like poetry, that is why I read it.

It does not matter if you do not understand it – *Savitri*, read it always. You will see that every time you read it, something new will be revealed to you. Each time you will get a new glimpse, each time a new experience; things which were not there, things you did not understand arise and suddenly become clear. Always an unexpected vision comes up through the words and lines. Every time you try to read and understand, you will see that something is added, something which was hidden behind is revealed clearly and vividly. I tell you the very verses you have read once before, will appear to you in a different light each time you re-read them. This is what happens invariably. Always your experience is enriched, it is a revelation at each step.

But you must not read it as you read other books or newspapers. You must read with an empty head, a blank and vacant mind, without there being any other thought; you must concentrate much, remain empty, calm and open; then the words, rhythms, vibrations will penetrate directly to this white page, will put their stamp upon the brain, will explain themselves without your making any effort.

Savitri alone is sufficient to make you climb to the highest peaks. If truly one knows how to meditate on *Savitri,* one will receive all the help one needs. For him who wishes to follow this path, it is a concrete help as though the Lord himself were taking you by the hand and leading you to the destined goal. And then, every question, however personal it may be, has its answer here, every difficulty finds its solution herein; indeed there is every thing that is necessary for doing the Yoga.

He has crammed the whole universe in a single book. It is a marvellous work, magnificent and of an incomparable perfection.

You know, before writing *Savitri* Sri Aurobindo said to me, I am impelled to launch on a new adventure; I was hesitant in the beginning, but now I am decided. Still I do not know how far I shall succeed. I pray for help. And you know what it was? It was – before beginning, I warn you in advance – it was His way of speaking, so full of divine humility and modesty. He never... asserted Himself. And the day He actually began it, He told me: I have launched myself in a rudderless boat upon the vastness of the Infinite. And once having started He wrote page after page without intermission, as though it were a thing already complete up there and He had only to transcribe it in ink down here on these pages.

In truth, the entire form of *Savitri* has descended " en masse" from the highest region and Sri Aurobindo with His genius only arranged the lines – in a superb and magnificent style. Sometimes entire lines were revealed and He has left them intact; He worked hard, untiringly, so that the inspiration could come from the highest possible summit. And what a work He has created! Yes, it is a true creation in itself. It is an unequalled work. Everything is there, and it is put in such a simple, such a clear form; verses perfectly harmonious, limpid and eternally true. My child, I have read so many things, but I have never come across anything which could be compared with *Savitri*. I have studied the best works in Greek, Latin, English and of course in French literature, also in German and all the great creations of the West and the East, including the great epics; but I repeat it, I have not found anywhere anything comparable with *Savitri*. All these literary works seem to me empty, flat, hollow, without any deep reality – apart from a few rare exceptions and these too represent only a small fraction of what *Savitri* is. What grandeur, what amplitude, what reality: it is something immortal and eternal He has created. I tell you once again there is nothing like it in the whole world. Even if one puts aside the vision of the reality, that is, the essential substance which is the heart of the inspiration, and considers only the lines in themselves one will find them unique, of the highest classical kind. What He has created is something man cannot imagine. For, everything is there, everything.

It may then be said that *Savitri* is a revelation, it is a meditation, it is a quest of the Infinite, the Eternal. If it is read with this aspiration for Immortality, the reading itself will serve as a guide to Immortality. To read *Savitri* is indeed to practise Yoga, spiritual concentration; one can find there all that is needed to realise the Divine. Each step of Yoga is noted here, including the secret of all other Yogas. Surely, if one sincerely follows what is revealed here in each line one will reach finally the transformation of the Supramental Yoga. lt is truly the infallible guide who never abandons you; its support is always there for him who wants to follow the path. Each verse of *Savitri* is like a revealed Mantra which surpasses all that man possessed by way of knowledge, and I repeat this, the words are expressed and arranged in such a way that the sonority of the rhythm leads you to the origin of sound, which is OM.

My child, yes, everything is there: mysticism, occultism, philosophy, the history of evolution, the history of man, of the gods, of creation, of Nature. How the universe was created, why, for what purpose, what destiny – all is there. You can find all the answers to all your questions there. Everything is explained, even the future of man and of the evolution, all that nobody yet knows. He has described it all in beautiful and clear words so that spiritual adventurers who wish to solve the mysteries of the world may understand it more easily. But this mystery is well hidden behind the words and lines and one must rise to the required level of true consciousness to discover it. All prophecies, all that is going to come is presented with a precise and wonderful clarity. Sri Aurobindo gives you here the key to find the Truth, to discover the Consciousness, to solve the problem of what the universe is. He has also indicated how to open the door of the Inconscience so that the light may penetrate there and transform it. He has shown the path, the way to liberate oneself from the ignorance and climb up to the superconscience; each stage, each plane of consciousness, how they can be scaled, how one can cross even the barrier to death and attain immortality. You will find the whole journey in detail, and as you go forward you can discover things altogether unknown to man. That is *Savitri*, and much more yet. It is a real experience – reading *Savitri*. All the secrets that man possessed, He has revealed, – as well as all that awaits him in the future; all this is found in the depth of *Savitri*. But one must have the knowledge to discover it all, the experience of the planes of consciousness, the experience of the Supermind, even the experience of the conquest of Death. He has noted all the stages, marked each step in order to advance integrally in the integral Yoga.

All this is His own experience, and what is most surprising is that it is my own experience also. It is my sadhana which He has worked out. Each object, each event, each realisation, all the descriptions, even the colours are exactly what I saw and the words, phrases are also exactly what I heard. And all this before having read the book. I read *Savitri* many times afterwards, but earlier, when He was writing He used to read it to me. Every morning I used to hear Him read *Savitri*. During the night He would write and in the morning read it to me. And I observed something curious, that day after day the experiences He read out to me in the morning were those I had had the previous night, word by word. Yes, all the descriptions, the colours, the pictures I had seen, the words I had heard, all, all, I heard it all, put by Him into poetry, into miraculous poetry. Yes, they were exactly my experiences of the previous night which He read out to me the following morning. And it was not just one day by chance, but for days and days together. And every time I used to compare what He said with my previous experiences and they were always the same. I repeat, it was not that I had told Him my experiences and that He had noted them down afterwards, no, He knew already what I had seen. It is my experiences He has presented at length and they were His experiences also. It is, moreover, the picture of Our joint adventure into the unknown or rather into the Supermind.

14

These are experiences lived by Him, realities, supracosmic truths. He experienced all these as one experiences joy or sorrow, physically. He walked in the darkness of inconscience, even in the neighbourhood of death, endured the sufferings of perdition, and emerged from the mud, the world-misery to breathe the sovereign plenitude and enter the supreme Ananda. He crossed all these realms, went through the consequences, suffered and endured physically what one cannot imagine. Nobody till today has suffered like Him. He accepted suffering to transform suffering into the joy of union with the Supreme. It is something unique and incomparable in the history of the world. It is something that has never happened before. He is the first to have traced the path in the Unknown, so that we may be able to walk with certitude towards the Supermind. He has made the work easy for us. *Savitri* is His whole Yoga of transformation, and this Yoga appears now for the first time in the earth- consciousness.

And I think that man is not yet ready to receive it. It is too high and too vast for him. He cannot understand it, grasp it, for it is not by the mind that one can understand *Savitri*. One needs spiritual experiences in order to understand and assimilate it. The farther one advances on the path of Yoga, the more does one assimilate and the better. No, it is something which will be appreciated only in the future, it is the poetry of tomorrow of which He has spoken in *The Future Poetry*. It is too suble, too refined, – it is not in the mind or through the mind, it is in meditation that *Savitri* is revealed.

And men have the audacity to compare it with the work of Virgil or Homer and to find it inferior. They do not understand, they cannot understand. What do they know? Nothing at all. And it is useless to try to make them understand. Men will know what it is, but in a distant future. It is only the new race with the new consciousness which will be able to understand. I assure you there is nothing under the blue sky to compare with *Savitri*. It is the mystery of mysteries. It is a super-epic, it is super-literature, super-poetry, supervision, it is a super-work even if one considers the number of lines He has written. No, these human words are not adequate to describe *Savitri*. Yes, one needs superlatives, hyperboles to describe it. It is a hyper-epic. No, words express nothing of what *Savitri* is, at least I do not find them. It is of immense value – spiritual value and all other values; it is eternal in its subject; and infinite in its appeal, miraculous in its mode and power of execution, it is a unique thing, the more you come in contact with it, the higher will you be uplifted. Ah, truly it is something! It is the most beautiful thing He has left for man, the highest possible. What is it? When will man know it? When is he going to lead a life of truth? When is he going to accept this in his life; This yet remains to be seen.

My child, everyday you are going to read Savitri; read properly, with the right attitude, concentrating a little before opening the pages and trying to keep the mind as empty as possible, absolutely without a thought. The direct road is

15

through the heart. I tell you, if you try to really concentrate with this aspiration you can light the flame, the psychic flame, the flame of purification in a very short time, perhaps in a few days. What you cannot do normally, you can do with the help of *Savitri*. Try and you will see how very different it is, how new, if you read with this attitude, with this something at the back of your consciousness; as though it were an offering to Sri Aurobindo. You know it is charged, fully charged with consciousness; as if *Savitri* were a being, a real guide. I tell you, whoever, wanting to practise Yoga, tries sincerely and feels the necessity for it, will be able to climb with the help of *Savitri* to the highest rung of the ladder of Yoga, will be able to find the secret that *Savitri* represents. And this without the help of a Guru. And he will be able to practise it anywhere. For him *Savitri* alone will be the guide, for all that he needs he will find in *Savitri*. If he remains very quiet when before a difficulty, or when he does not know where to turn to go forward and how to overcome obstacles, for all these hesitations and incertitudes which overwhelm us at every moment, he will have the necessary indications, and the necessary concrete help. If he remains very calm, open, if he aspires sincerely, always he will be as if led by the hand. If he has faith, the will to give himself and essential sincerity he will reach the final goal.

Indeed, *Savitri* is something concrete, living, it is all replete, packed with consciousness, it is the supreme knowledge above all human philosophies and religions. It is the spiritual Path, it is Yoga, Tapasya, Sadhana, everything, in its single body. *Savitri* has an extraordinary power, it gives out vibrations for him who can receive them, the true vibrations of each stage of consciousness. It is incomparable, it is truth in its plenitude, the Truth Sri Aurobindo brought down on the earth. My child, one must try to find the secret that *Savitri* represents, the prophetic message Sri Aurobindo reveals there for us. This is the work before you, it is hard but it is worth the trouble.

Blessings

(A conversation of the Mother with Mona Sarkar recorded by him from memory)

'Sri Aurobindo Society Baroda - 21-2-1984'

SAVITRI the supreme revelation of
Sri Aurobindo's Vision.

The Mother

16

INDIA AND THE WORLD

One sees that the world in general is at present in a sort of disequilibrium and chaos. Does this mean that it is preparing itself for the manifestation of a new force, for the descent of the Truth? Or is this the result of the action of hostile forces in revolt against this descent? And what place does India occupy in all this?

It is both at the same time. It is a chaotic means of preparation. India should be the spiritual guide explaining what is happening and helping to shorten the movement? But, unfortunately, in her blind ambition to imitate the West, she has become materialistic and neglectful of her soul.

13.10.1965

India is supposed to be the Guru of the world in order to establish the spiritual life on earth. But, Mother, in order to occupy this high position she must be worthy politically, morally and physically, must she not?

Without any doubt and for the present, there is much to be done!

07.09.1966

Why this chaotic condition in our present government? Is it the sign of the change for the good, for the reign of Truth?

It is the pressure upon the entire earth of the force of Truth which causes disorder, confusion and falsehood to Spring up everywhere in a refusal to be transformed.

The way of the Truth is certain, but it is difficult to say when and how it will come about.

14.09.1966

Mother, l have heard that in 1967 India will become "the spiritual Guru of the world". But how? When we consider the present condition.

India ought to be the spiritual leader of the world. Inside she has the capacity, but outside ... for the moment there is still much to do for her to become actually the spiritual leader of the world.

08.08.1967

There is such a wonderful opportunity just now! but India has become the symbolic representation of all the difficulties of modern mankind India will be the land of its resurrection the resurrection to a higher and truer life. That same thing which, in the history of the universe, made the earth the symbolic representation of the universe so as to be able to concentrate the work on one point, the same

17

phenomenon is taking place now: India represents all the terrestrial human difficulties, and it is in India that there will be the cure. And it is for this, it is for this that I have been made to start Auroville.

03.02.1968

Years ago, at the time when Sri Aurobindo was here, there was the vision, an inner vision, that India was the place where the destiny of the earth would be decided.

So there are two opposite possibilities. It was, as if it was said, that if there was a war, it was India where it would take place; that the world conflict, the game would be played in India. But will the Force of Peace be sufficient to prevent the war? The whole question lies there. But it is here where the whirlwind of forces is, above India.

It is like a conflict between the forces that wish to destroy the earth and the terrestrial transformation. If these forces can be checked, can be mastered and made powerless, then the terrestrial progress and transformation are going to proceed straight and quickly magnificent! But at present it is like monsters coming from all sides to obstruct.

19.04.1969

"DIARY 2000"

The 15th August 1945

The Victory has come, Thy Victory, O Lord, for which we render to Thee infinite thanks-giving.

But now our ardent prayer rises towards Thee. It is with Thy force and by Thy force that the victors have conquered. Grant that they do not forget it in their success and that they keep the promises which they have made to Thee in the hours of danger and anguish. They have taken Thy name to make war, may they not forget Thy grace when they have to make the peace.

YOGA, SEX, FOOD, AND SLEEP
Sri Aurobindo

Q: Is it true that sexual desire is the greatest obstacle in Yoga ?

A: One of the greatest, at least.

Q: Does sexual desire increase by taking more food and decrease by taking less ?

A: It is rather certain kinds of food that are supposed to increase it – e.g., meat, onions, chillies, etc.

Q: Are greed, anger, jealousy etc., the companions of the sexual desire ?

A: They usually go with sexual desire, though not always.

Q: The Mother has said: "the strength of such impulses as those of the sex lies usually in the fact that people take too much notice of them". What is meant by a person taking too much notice of these impulses ?

A: If he is always thinking of them and struggling with them, that is taking too much notice.

Q: What should he do to avoid taking too much notice ?

A: He has to detach himself from them, think less of sex and more of the Divine.

Q: The Mother has also said in regard to sexual thoughts that it is wrong to "endeavour to control them by coercion, hold them within and sit upon them". How does a person hold these thoughts within and sit upon them ?

A: The words convey their own explanation. If you remain full of sexual thoughts and try to prevent them from manifesting in some kind of action, that is holding them within and sitting on them. It is the same with anger or any other passion. They have to be thrown away, not kept in you.

Q: You have said that the control of a wrong movement merely suppresses it and that to remove it completely it has to be rejected. What is the utility then of controlling movements of sex, anger, fear, etc.

A: If your rejection is not successful, you have to control. The control at least prevents you from being the slave of your vital impulses. Once you have the control, it is easier to reject successfully. Absence of control does not bring successful rejection.

Q: What is the process of turning the sexual energy into 'ojas' ?

A: If it is to be done by a process, it will have to be by Tapasya (self-control of mind, speech, act) and a drawing upward of the seminal energy through the will. But it can be better done by the descent of the Force and its working on the sex-centre and consequent transformation, as with all other things in this Yoga.

Q: Is fasting a help in our sadhana ?

A: This sadhana is not helped by fasting.

Q: Is taking very little food helpful in controlling the senses ?

A: No, it simply exasperates them—to take a moderate amount is best. People who fast easily get exalted and may lose their balance.

Q: If one takes only vegetarian food, does it help in controlling the senses ?

A: It avoids some of the difficulties which the meat-eaters have, but it is not sufficient by itself.

Q: Is sleep necessary for a sadhak who has reached the higher consciousness ?

A: So long as one has a body that is not altogether transformed in all its functionings, sleep is necessary.

Q: Why are the mind and vital so active at night ? How could one control their activity at night ?

A: It is their function. So long as one is not perfectly conscious in sleep, they will act.

Q: In the first and middle part of my sleep there is a great mental and vital activity but in the last part this activity subsides and I get various kinds of symbolic dreams and intimations of higher knowledge. What is the reason of this?

A: In sleep one very commonly passes from consciousness to deeper consciousness in a long succession until one reaches the psychic and test there or else from higher to higher consciousness until one reaches rest in some silence and peace. The few minutes one passes in this rest are the real sleep which restores,–if one does not get it, there is only a half rest. It is when you come near to either of these domains of rest that you begin to see these higher kinds of dreams.

Q: What is the way to pass into the psychic or higher consciousness in sleep and rest there ?

A: It is done unconsciously as it is. If one wants to do it consciously and regulate it, one has first to become conscious in sleep.

Q: How to make a heavy sub-conscient sleep light ?

A: By calling in more consciousness.

Q: I have noticed that even half an hour's sleep during day-time refreshes me more than five or six hour's sleep at night. What is the reason for this ?

A: It must be because it is a different kind of sleep in the day-times, less heavy, with less time spent in the subconscient.

Q: Some people say that they have dreamless sleep for the whole night. Is this possible ?

A: They simply mean that when they are not conscious of having dreamed. In the sleep the consciousness goes into other planes and has experiences there and when these are translated perfectly or imperfectly by the physical mind, they are called dreams. All the time of sleep such dreams take place, but sometimes one remembers and at other times does not at all remember. Sometimes also one goes low down into the subconscient and the dreams are there, but so deep down that when one comes out there is not even the consciousness that one had dreamed.

Q: Have dreams any significance ? Is there any meaning in the dreams of the subconscient ?

A: A dream, when it is not from the subconscient, is either symbolic or else an experience of some supraphysical plane or a formation therein by some mental or vital or other force or in rare cases an indication of some event actual or probable in the past, present or future. A dream from the subconscious plane has no meaning; it is simply a *khichadi* of impressions and memories left in the subconscient from the past.

Q: In a dream I saw some people climbing up a mountain with great difficulty. I was also climbing with them. After a time I got tired, so I gave up climbing and began to think what was to be done. Then I felt that a force lifted me up lightly and carried me to the top of the mountain. On reaching the top, I saw that there were many beautiful houses of different colours and lights. Then I woke up. What does this dream signify ?

A: It is a symbol of the two methods — one of self-effort, the other of the action of the Mother's Force carrying the sadhak.

Q: During sleep I often get bad dreams of the vital plane. How to prevent this ?

A: You can do it by having a will in the waking state against these things coming in the dream, before you go to sleep for instance. It will not succeed at once but it will in the end. Or else you must aspire to grow more conscious in sleep.

Q: Sometimes when I have an attack in dream, I can get rid of it by repeating the Mother's name. Does this mean that even the Mother's name has power in it?

A: Yes, certainly, there is always a power in the Name.

'Srivantu' 15 August 1968

From: Elements of Yoga

"Man" and "The Divine"

A disciple: Mother, who am I?

The Divine under many disguises.

*

Q: What is God?

God is the perfection that we must aspire to realise.

*

For those who are afraid of a word:

This is what we mean by "Divine": all the knowledge we have to acquire, all the power we have to obtain, all the love we have to become, all the perfection we have to achieve, all the harmonious and progressive poise we have to manifest in light and joy, all the new and unknown splendours that have to be realised.

*

With regard to the Truth, we are all divine; but we hardly know it. And in us, it is precisely that which does not know itself as divine which we call "ourselves".

*

Q: Mother, are you God?

This question can be asked of any human being. And the answer is: Yes, potentially.

And the task of each one is to make it a real fact.

THE MOTHER

AIM July 1987

Spiritual Life
(Compiled from notes and letters of Sri Aurobindo)

Sri Aurobindo began his practice of yoga in 1904. Even before this, several experiences had come to him spontaneously, "of themselves and with a sudden unexpectedness". There was, for instance, the mental experience of the *atman* or true Self, which he had while reading the Upanishads in London in 1892. The next year a "vast calm" descended upon him the moment he stepped on Indian soil after his long absence in England. This calm surrounded him and remained for many months afterwards. Also in 1893 Sri Aurobindo had a vision of the Godhead surging up from within when he was in danger of a carriage accident. In 1903, while walking on the ridge of the Takht-i-Suleman in Kashmir, he had the "realisation of the vacant Infinite", and a year or two later he experienced the "living presence of Kali" in a shrine on the banks of the Narmada.

In 1904 Sri Aurobindo began yoga with the "assiduous practice of *pranayama*". Around this time he met the yogi Brahmananda and was "greatly impressed by him", but he had no helper or guru in yoga until January 1908, when he met the Maharashtrian yogi Vishnu Bhaskar Lele. Lele showed Sri Aurobindo how to establish complete silence of mind and immobility of consciousness. Within three days Sri Aurobindo succeeded in achieving this state that sometimes requires a lifetime of yoga to attain. The result was a series of "lasting and massive spiritual realisations which opened to him the larger ways of yoga"; Lele finally told Sri Aurobindo to put himself entirely into the hands of the Divine within and to move only as he was moved by Him. This henceforward became the whole foundation and principle of Sri Aurobindo's sadhana. Sri Aurobindo and Lele parted ways after a month or two, and from this time until the Mother came to India Sri Aurobindo received no spiritual help from anyone.

In 1908 and 1909, while Sri Aurobindo was an undertrial prisoner in the Alipur Jail, he had the constant vision of the omnipresent Godhead: "I looked at the jail that secluded me from men and it was no longer by its high walls that I was imprisoned; no, it was Vasudeva who surrounded me. I walked under the branches of the tree in front of my cell, but it was not a tree, I knew it was Vasudeva, it was Sri Krishna whom I saw standing there and holding over me his shade. I looked at the bars of my cell, the very grating that did duty for a door and again I saw Vasudeva. It was Narayana who was guarding and standing sentry over me. Or I lay on the coarse blankets that were given me for a couch and felt the arms of Sri Krishna around me, the arms of my Friend and Lover...."

But this did not mean, as most people supposed, that he had retired into, some height of spiritual experience devoid of any further interest in the world or in the fate of India. It could not mean that, for the very principle of his Yoga was not only to realise the Divine and attain to a complete spiritual consciousness, but also to take all life and all world activity into the scope of this spiritual consciousness and action and to base life on the spirit and give it a spiritual meaning. In his retirement Sri Aurobindo kept a close watch on all that was happening in the world and in India and actively intervened whenever necessary, but solely with a spiritual force and silent spiritual action; for it is part of the experience of those who have advanced far in yoga that besides the ordinary forces and activities of the mind and life and body in Matter, there are other forces and powers that can act and do act from behind and from above; there is also a spiritual dynamic power which can be possessed by those who are advanced in the spiritual consciousness, though all do not care to possess or, possessing, to use it and this power is greater than any other and more effective. It was this force, which, as soon as he attained to it, he used, at first only in a limited field of personal work, but afterwards in a constant action upon the world forces. He had no reason to be dissatisfied with the results or to feel the necessity of any other kind of action. Twice however he found it advisable to take in addition other action of a public kind. The first was in relation to the Second World War. At the beginning he did not actively concern himself with it, but when it appeared as if Hitler would crush all the forces opposed to him and Nazism dominate the world, he began to intervene. He declared himself publicly on the side of the Allies, made some financial contributions in answer to the appeal for funds and encouraged those who sought his advice to enter the army or share in the war effort. Inwardly, he put his spiritual force behind the Allies from the moment of Dunkirk when everybody was expecting the immediate fall of England and the definite triumph of Hitler, and he had the satisfaction of seeing the rush of German victory almost immediately arrested and the tide of war begin to turn in the opposite direction. This he did, because he saw that behind Hitler and Nazism were dark Asuric forces and that their success would mean the enslavement of mankind to the tyranny of evil, and a set-back to the course of evolution and especially to the spiritual evolution of mankind: it would lead also to the enslavement not only of Europe but of Asia, and in it India, an enslavement far more terrible than any this country had ever endured, and the undoing of all the work that had been done for her liberation. It was this reason also that induced him to support publicly the Cripps' offer and to press the Congress leaders to accept it. He had not, for various reasons, intervened with his spiritual force against the Japanese aggression until it became evident that Japan intended to attack and even invade and conquer India. He allowed certain letters he had written in support of the war affirming his views of the Asuric nature and inevitable outcome of Hitlerism to become public. He supported the Cripps' offer because by its acceptance India and Britain could stand united against the Asuric (hostile) forces and the solution of Cripps could be used as a step towards independence.

Courtesy *"SRI AUROBINDO AND HIS ASHRAM"*

Divine Incarnation

Nagin Doshi's[1] Correspondence with Sri Aurobindo

Q: What is an incarnation ?

An incarnation is the Divine Consciousness and Being manifesting through the body.

Q: When the Divine descends here as an incarnation, does not that very act mould his infinity into a limited finite? How then does he still continue to rule over the universe?

Do you imagine that the Divine is at any time not everywhere in the universe or beyond it? or that he is living at one point in space and governing the rest from it, as Mussolini governs the Italian Empire from Rome?

Q: I was speaking of the Divine in the body, and not of the Divine in his supreme plane above in an impersonal and formless aspect. Does not his incarnation on earth necessarily limit him ? Living in such a world he has to govern all the three universes!

It is the omnipresent cosmic Divine who supports the action of the universe; if there is an Incarnation, it does not in the least diminish the cosmic Presence and the cosmic action in the three or thirty million universes.

Q: When the Avatar comes down here how does he take on a mind, vital and body? It is, I think, the soul that is divine, but the adhar has to be built up from the cosmos?

Everybody has to do that when he is born. It is the soul that is permanent.

Q: Does an Avatar create a new mind, life and body from the cosmos for himself or take hold of some liberated human being and use his outer personality for his manifestation ?

That would be a possession not an Avatar. An Avatar is supposed to be from birth. Each soul at its birth takes from the cosmic mind, life and matter to shape a new external personality for himself. What prevents the Divine doing the same? What is continued from birth to birth is the inner being.

Q: You wrote: "The Avatar is a special manifestation, while for the rest of the time it is the Divine working with the ordinary human limits as a Vibhuti." Does not the Divine find it difficult to mould himself into a Vibhuti and accept the human limits?

---

1. Nagin Doshi came to the Ashram in 1931 when he was a boy of fourteen years. The present selection is from his correspondence with Sri Aurobindo during 1933-34.

Why should it be difficult? Even the Avatar accepts limits for his work.

Q: Since an Avatar comes here with a divine Power, Light and Ananda why should he pass through the same process of sadhana as an ordinary sadhak?

The Avatar is not supposed to act in a non-human way - he takes up human action and uses human methods with the human consciousness in front and the Divine behind. If he did not his taking a human body would have no meaning and would be of no use to anybody. He could just as well have stayed above and done things from there.

Q: The Avatar, unlike the Vibhuti, does not need to satisfy his vital. [Sri Aurobindo's marginal remark: "Why should he not?"] For his vital has no cravings and desires as our vital has. He is above them. And if he seems to be satisfying them, it is only to acquire experience and knowledge of the vital worlds.

All that is wrong. The Avatar takes upon himself the nature of humanity in his instrumental parts, through the consciousness acting behind is divine.

Q: When the Divine descends here (as the Avatar), he has to veil himself and deal with the world and its movements like an ordinary man of the cosmic product [Sri Aurobindo's marginal remark: "Exactly"]. But behind he is perfectly conscious of what happens. The universal forces cannot make him their tool as they make us.

That does not prevent the Avatar from acting as men act and using the movements of Nature for his life and work.

'Nagin Doshi's Correspondence with Sri Aurobindo'

* * * * * * * * *

A Prayer

O Lord, I pray to thee,
Guide my footsteps, enlighten my mind.
That at every moment
And in all things I may
Do exactly what thou wantest me to do.

The Mother

How to do yoga?

Shri Nirodbaran once wrote to Sri Aurobindo' "Please give me some necessary instructions, not depending on my notes, as to what should be done. If I have seen the tail it must lead me to the head!"

Sri Aurobindo replied (26 March 1937):

"There is nothing to do but to go on concentrating and calling the Presence within and without you, the opening, the power to receive and let it come. The more the mind falls quiet during or as the result of concentration, the better (no other thought in or out). But no need to struggle for that, must come of itself by the concentration."

Shri Udar Pinto states: "I joined the Sri Aurobindo Ashram in 1937 and since then I have tried to do His Yoga as best I could by reading the very fine books He has written on this matter. But after about 25 years or more of this effort I was not at all sure that I had reached anywhere and so one day I told this to our Sweet Mother and asked Her if I was doing the Yoga correctly. I really hoped for Her Blessings to help me do it correctly but I got a shock when She said that I was doing it all wrong. I was nonplussed and asked Her what I should do and She answered, smiling: 'Why do you want to do the Yoga and do it all wrong?' I said: 'Then what to do?' She replied: 'I will do the Yoga for you! You can stop all you are doing and let me do it. I have come down on earth to make things easy for you so why should you try when I am here to do it?' I asked 'What then is my part?' 'Just give yourself to me and I will do it all for you and you just go on doing the work you are doing for me.' I accepted at once and I shook the hand of the Mother as a sign of the contract we formed that day.

"But then I found that giving oneself to The Mother is easy to say but so difficult to do and so I asked Her how to do it. She said: 'In the morning when you get up what do you do?' I said I do my toilet and get ready for my bath. But She asked for detail and I said I started with brushing my teeth. Then She asked: 'But what do you think of or dream about when you brush your teeth?' And I said that it was such a usual thing to do that I found nothing to think about or to dream about. Then She told me what I should do during each act of my toilet, my bath, my breakfast, etc. She said, 'Feel my presence very much with you. Make me do with you the things you are doing. Talk to me, discuss with me the best way of doing what you have to do. While eating, let us together find the wonderful taste of what we are eating. You will see how wonderful will taste even a slice of bread if you eat it with me, together, enjoying its taste.' So now I try to do this and it has changed my whole life and has made everything so beautiful and full of joy."

Shri Navajata spoke thus, at a public meeting held in January 1981: "One of the greatest problems of man, in both life and yoga, is to have communion with the Divine, to build a line of communication by which he can receive the guidance and act accordingly. Man does not know that he does not have to build the line of communication, he does not have to do communion himself. The Divine builds the line of communication, the Divine reaches out to you. He puts your consciousness in order, He says what has to be said and does whatever has to be done. Only, you have to get plugged in to Him, you have to just switch on to Him. That is the only thing needed from your side. All the rest He does.

"That is what Sri Aurobindo has said: *All would change if man could once consent to be spiritualised.* So the main thing is your consent. 'I want to change, I want to be perfect, I want to be divinised', and to put yourself in His hands in a very open and sincere manner. All your desires, all your preferences, the desire even to serve humanity, the desire even to do good, come in the way of your opening to the Divine, of your switching on to Him.

"The best thing I can advise you from a very practical angle is, when you get up in the morning, spend half an hour with the Divine. Make it a rule of your life: 'I want to spend at least half an hour with Him, just with Him'. Whatever be your concept of Him, whatever be your shortcomings, your hesitations, doubts, lack of confidence as to how there could be any easy way to establish a communion or communication with Him, despite all these, make a resolution: I want to spend half an hour with the Divine everyday in the morning, I want to talk to Him, put my problems before Him, put my aspirations before Him, just as I would put them to somebody dearest and closest to me, with the faith that the Divine is Omniscient and Omnipotent and that He will hear. Try it for one day and see the result; for one day and you will know what happens to you and what can happen to you. Just half an hour one day. And if you do this properly for one day, you will want to do it the whole day, the whole night, and the next day and all your life.

"For those of you who are ready, who really feel the need to be guided by Him, really feel the need to be perfect, this is the first and decisive step to take to establish unity with the Divine. You know, in our consciousness there are, established from childhood, from-birth and from even previous lives, a number of 'samskáráh' in the mental plane, which obstruct our communication with the Divine. But once we have established this rapport, He puts them right, He cleans them away and everything then becomes different for us. So, you must know that this is the simplest way to solve the difficulties; every other way is of great tapasya, of great effort. But this kind of communication with Him, communion with Him, will help you realise how He puts things right in your consciousness.

"When you talk to Him, you will be surprised to find that even the imperfections in your thoughts disappear, the imperfections of your aspirations disappear, these will simply vanish. You will feel that what you are trying to talk to Him is imperfect, it has to take another shape.

"So this is what I would like to tell you very briefly: learn to communicate with the Divine and be with Him at least for half an hour every day. And this is the best contact you can have during the twenty-four hours, the half an hour you spend with Him. So on this occasion, I invoke the special Blessings of the Mother and Sri Aurobindo for all of you that you may open to the Supramental Light and Force. May Sri Aurobindo's Consciousness awaken, and settle in your mind, life and body, and manifest itself so that each one of you can become a radiating centre of His Presence and His Manifestation. May His Blessings be with you."

'AIM' July 1995

28

DYUMAN'S CORRESPONDENCE WITH THE MOTHER

My dear Mother,

Unless the body consciousness opens and receives the Divine Light, Peace and Consciousness, nothing of permanence is achieved. The body is the base, and upon that base the Divine has to work and construct a building. However much the vital and the mental are open and receptive, nothing can be said to be permanent if the body is not stable.

I AM glad that you had the experience of the necessity for the body to open and to receive the divine Light and Will, as the mind and the heart does. This will do much for the increase of the resistance to illness and the capacity of keeping good health.

I am always with you.

15 May 1935

My dear Mother,

I am always given to Thee and to Thy Work. Make me more quiet, make me rest in full peace amidst these hundredfold activities. I have to learn this more and more, and You have to teach me. Teach me, my dear Mother, to be more and more Thine.

Yes, I am always with you, teaching you the true action and the true consecration.

19 May 1935

My dear Mother,

The most important thing for me to do is to remain quietly happy, consecrated and concentrated on You, and to do what has to be done very sincerely and devotionally, not worrying about the future, but quietly aspiring very humbly before You.

Yes, this is the right attitude and the most sure way.
Always with you in an affectionate trust.

27 May 1935

My dear Mother,

What did I see this evening when You were looking at me from Your window? I saw that my chest was as transparent as glass and that You were seeing Your own image there.

My dear Mother is always in my heart for eternity. My Mother; my Mother, my Mother.

This is a very beautiful and true experience. I am happy you had it. Yes, I am always in your heart – forever with you.

28 May 1935

My dear Mother,
    I fail to understand why there is so much antipathy against me in the Aroumé workers.

I do not think it is so bad as all that.

Three days back, as soon as I entered the Aroumé gate from the market, a force ran through my neck, saying: "It would have been better if you had died."

Do not listen to all this rubbish. *It does not come from the Aroumé workers,* but from some hostile force that wants to upset you.

Yesterday when I was taking my lunch, a force wanted to send me away from Aroumé: "Go away, go away, you are not wanted here."

Same explanation as above.

And now B tells me: "I shall not be able to cooperate with you in this way, nor shall I be able to work with you." I do not even know what "way" he means.
    My dear Mother, all is left to you. I rest happily and go to bed.

Yes, be quiet and do not worry about all that.
    It is the same forces which want to make you believe that your co-workers hate you and make the others believe that you hate them. The mistake is to believe these forces – one ought always to answer them: *No, it is not true, it cannot be.*
    Always with you, my dear child.

30 May 1935

My dear Mother,
    I thought that as I have grown bulky, I might not be able to work physically. But I find that I can work with a sustained energy, quietly and with a balanced mind. And I think You are quite happy to see me working.

Yes, I am very glad to see you working physically and am sure it will do you much good. I am glad also that your body is getting a little less thin. It was truly necessary to fill the holes!
    All love and blessings to you, my dear child.

30 May 1935

My dear Mother,

Today I heard C and D quarrelling. Afterwards, F told someone: "Prison life is easier than to work with C."

Would it not be better if you spoke to D? If he is not satisfied, it is better for him to tell it frankly rather than to complain hidingly.

Always with you, my dear child.

1 June 1935

My dear Mother,

I have spoken to D very clearly: "Give dumb-service; utter not a word even if there are whips on your back."

If you mean that there must be no quarrels it is quite all right. But he must feel free to tell me what he has in his heart.

"Work can never be done if there is no discipline! The Mother knows very well the person in charge of the work, and those who work with him have to follow his instructions." And he has agreed to that kind of work.

Let us see, my dear Mother. I wish that dumb service should be given to You by all of us.

I wanted you to tell him also that if he has any complaint to make or if he is not satisfied with his work, it is *to me* that he must freely say so.

My love, blessings and trust are always with you, my dear child.

2 June 1935

"Mother India" April 1998

Always behave as if the Mother was looking at you; because she is, indeed, always present.

Sri Aurobindo

This is not a mere phrase, not simply words, it is a fact. I am with you in a very concrete manner and they who have a *subtle* vision can see me.

The Mother

31

SECTION II

Interviews

The Mother on Corrections in *Savitri*

An interview with Amal Kiran on 8 June 1999

According to your book Our Light and Delight *[p. 23], the Mother once told you, "I won't allow you to change even a comma in Savitri." Is this true?*

AMAL: Yes, but she meant I could not change anything according to my own ideas. After that I made it clear to her that corrections would be only according to Sri Aurobindo's latest version. Some words had been misread and I had suggested what might be the right reading. But we would not dare to change anything on our own. I told her this. And Mother quite understood the situation. "That's a different matter," she said.

So she approved of my making my suggestions, and many of them were found to be correct when the manuscripts were checked.

Have you written about this anywhere?

AMAL: Part of it is there in *Our Light and Delight.* To anyone who reads it carefully, the Mother's attitude towards the correction of copying mistakes and such things should be clear enough.

But most of the conversation recorded there [*Our Light and Delight,* pp. 23-25] is not about such corrections at all. It is about a statement I wanted to include in the Publisher's Note. I wanted to say that certain passages in Parts II and III had not received Sri Aurobindo's final revision. The Mother's strong reaction to this has been quoted as if it showed that she was against correcting copying mistakes or typographical errors in *Savitri.* But she never objected to corrections of that kind. Naturally she wanted Sri Aurobindo's own words to be printed in *Savitri,* not a version with words accidentally substituted by others.

Later, the Mother even accepted the substance of what I had wanted to write in the Publisher's Note. She agreed to have it included in the Note before the letters at the end of the 1954 edition. It was only something in my attitude that had provoked her reaction. This was her way of working. It brought about a great change in me.

Extracts from *Our Light and Delight* by Amal Kiran

. . . when the second volume of the first edition of *Savitri* was under preparation, a sadhak had stressed to the Mother the danger of sending the proofs to me. The Mother seems even to have passed an order against sending them. But Prithwisingh and Nirod made urgent representations to her, saying that it would be a great mistake not to let me see the proofs, for I had made very appropriate suggestions in the past, which had been found correct when the typed copy had been compared with the original manuscript. So the Mother cancelled her order but left, of course, the final decision in the hands of Nolini and Nirod. [p.23]

"Mother," I said, "I am not wanting you to sanction the changing of commas and such things. All I want is that in some sort of Publisher's Note we should say that certain passages in Parts II and III did not receive final revision: otherwise critics will think that they are what Sri Aurobindo intended them finally to be." [p. 24]

Some time afterwards, when I was putting together the letters which Sri Aurobindo had written to me on *Savitri* to serve as a supplement in the last part of the volume, I spoke to the Mother of an introductory note to them. She consented to listen to what I had a mind to write. In that note most of the points which I had previously put to her but which she had rejected came in again, amidst some other matters. She approved of all of them unconditionally. And when I proposed that this note might go as a footnote in small print she expressed her wish that it should go as a real introduction in its own right. [p. 27]

I have related elsewhere some other incidents connected with my editorial work on *Savitri*. I may here mention the grand finale, as it were. After the last pages had been printed, the Mother calmly announced to me: "The Press is very displeased with you." I answered: "I know it, Mother, and I am sorry I have troubled the Press. But are you displeased with my work?" She gave a faint smile and said: "No." [p. 212]

'On the New Edition of Savitri' Page 5-6-7

Interview to *India*

Sri Aurobindo had been in contact with *India* even before his decision to go to Pondicherry. In July 1909 he had met representatives of the Swadeshi Steamship Company. Srinivas Acharya's elder brother S. Thirumalachari was one of the backers of this pioneering Indian-run concern. It is not certain who the company's representatives were; but it is known that two relatives of Srinivas Acharya, his brother-in-law Rangacharya and his younger brother Parthasarathy Aiyengar, had each visited Sri Aurobindo in Calcutta. The writer of a life-sketch of Parthasarathy has even asserted that Sri Aurobindo's choice of Pondicherry as a place of refuge was the result of a suggestion made by the Tamil youth. When Parthasarathy heard about the police harassment Sri Aurobindo was undergoing, he "pointed out the advantages of Pondicherry", telling Sri Aurobindo that the French settlement might prove "congenial to his mission".

Shortly after this, Sri Aurobindo granted an interview to an unidentified correspondent of the Tamil newspaper *India*—possibly Rangacharya or Parthasarathy. Excerpts from this interview were published in its issue of September 18, 1909:

> When our correspondent saw Aravindar, the first thought that came to his mind, it seems, was, "Is this Aravindar?"... Aravindar is of a lean frame; and he was sitting like a very ordinary man with a piece of cloth thrown over his upper body.... It was when he saw the eyes that our correspondent felt reassured. Oh! how knowing those eyes were! What grace in them! What peace! Mahashanti, mahashanti! The room exuded a great sattwic shanti.

The correspondent began with questions about the vision of the omnipresent Divine (Narayana or Krishna) that Sri Aurobindo had experienced in Alipore jail.

> Since a *darshan* of the Supreme is a rarity in this age, our correspondent wondered whether Aravindar's *darshan* could have come about in the dream-state. But when he listened to Aravindar's reply, all his doubts vanished. When our correspondent saw the humility, the peace, the solemnity, the innocence and the light that appeared on Aravindar's face... it was very clear to him that Aravindar is indeed a Mahasiddha.
>
> Aravindar: Yes, I saw Narayana. I had all my *darshans* in the waking state; they were not dreams.

Asked about the yoga he had practised during his imprisonment, Sri Aurobindo replied:

34

It was Bhakti Yoga. Leave all responsibility to the Divine. Try to realize that whatever you think, speak, or do is not yours, and that it is the Divine who thinks, speaks and acts through you. The realization will come in time. Realization is different from vision. Crush your ego, be without the "I", practise self-renunciation.

The conversation moved on to the current political situation. Calcutta was "rife with the rumour" that Sri Aurobindo was going to be deported, but he knew that the Viceroy and his council had not accepted this suggestion "from the Calcutta police". When the correspondent expressed the faith that "God shall allow none to touch you, because you are destined to show the way to the nation for a while yet", Sri Aurobindo smiled.

As they talked, "a state of peace was born" in the correspondent's mind. "It gave me great bliss to think that I was in the presence of... one whose utterances have been the wonder of the whole nation... one of the Rishis of the Swadeshi Dharma. I was astonished to see him conversing with me calmly and peacefully even while his own brother was awaiting the death sentence." Finally, he asked Sri Aurobindo about "the present confused state of India". The reply:

There will be a *pralayam* [upheaval].... The year 1906 completes 5000 years of Kaliyuga, and a new age has begun with the year 1907. The upheaval will have developed well enough to be visible to all. It will be complete in a further period of four to five years....

The Mahapralayam will be one of a revolutionary change, a great step; the low will be raised and the high brought down. There will be change, change, everywhere – change in Government, change in our people; new resolves, new thoughts, new ways for all actions.

'Sri Aurobindo – His Life, Work and Teaching', page 26, 27, 28

THE HINDUSTAN TIMES: AUG 15,1952

Sri Aurobindo Ashram—A Pilgrimage

K.M. MUNSHI
(Governor of U.P.)

August 15. It is a wonderful day, the day when Freedom came, Sri Aurobindo was born, and Lokamanya left us the legacy of our birthright.

On March 12, 1952, I got off at the Madras station and went by car to Pondicherry. The Yuvaraja of-Pithapuram - a zamindar of Madras - joined me on this occasion, as on a previous one. Sri Aurobindo had come into the life of this good-natured man, who takes life as it comes cheerfully, in a curious way. Once he dreamt of a venerable old man. Months later, he went to Pondicherry where he had the darshan of the Master. At once he recognized the old man of his dreams and fell under his influence. Not that his life was suddenly transformed. Nor did he delve into the secrets of the 'Life Divine'. But he felt an unfamiliar but overpowering reverence towards Sri Aurobindo. A vein of hidden spirituality was opened in him and he got the solace he needed.

II

In the course of my life, I came in living touch with three Masters: Sri Aurobindo, Mrs. Besant and Gandhiji. Besant influenced me a little; Gandhiji intimately; Sri Aurobindo whose contact goes back to my boyhood, profoundly. I call all these three 'Masters'. When I say 'Masters' I do not wish to be accused of or honoured with being a devotee. Such persons become for me living commentaries on the perfect life. I absorb their influence; I bask in it; I feel refreshed but rarely do I change over to their way of life.To me, they are lighthouses of the Spirit. I steer my frail bark my own way, grateful for the light given to me.

Sri Aurobindo was my professor in the Baroda College, and his militant nationalism of 1904 moulded my early outlook. Later I casually read some of his works. During the last few years, however, his influence has been coming over me intermittently, but I have felt more and more perceptibly benefited by it. Often in the past I wanted to go to Pondicherry, but I did not wish to offer formal respects to a man whom I revered so deeply. In July 1950, however, I felt an urge to visit the Ashram. Normally, as you know, Sri Aurobindo did not see people, except on four days in the year. But in my case he told the Secretary, he treated me as a disciple and would make an exception.

When I visited him, after the lapse of more than 40 years, I saw before me a being completely transformed: radiant, blissful, enveloped in an atmosphere of godlike calm. He spoke in a low, clear voice, which stirred the depths of my being.

I talked to him of my spiritual needs. I said: "I am at a dead end. The world is too much with me."

The Sage replied: "You need not give up the world in order to advance in self-realisation. But you cannot advance by impatience. I wrote to you that I would help you, and in my own way I am helping you.... You have the urge and the light. Go your own way. Do not be deflected from the faith in your natural evolution. I will watch over your progress."

Then we discussed Indian culture, its present crisis, even the Hindu Code. When I said, "the younger generation is fed on theories and beliefs which are undermining the higher life of India," Sri Aurobindo replied: "You must overcome this lack of faith. Rest assured that our culture cannot be undermined. This is only a passing phase."

Then he sprang a surprise on me. "When do you expect India to be united?" he asked.

I was taken aback. I explained to him how our leaders had agreed to partition. "So long as the present generation of politicians is concerned, I cannot think of any time when the two countries – India and Pakistan – can be united."

The Master smiled. "India will be re-united. I see it clearly." Was it an opinion? Or a prophecy? Or was it clear perception?

I shook my head in doubt and asked how India could be re-united. In two short sentences he described what Pakistan stood for and indicated how the two countries could come together.

Knowing us politicians, I could do nothing but again shake my head sceptically.

Now we talked of Pondicherry. He told me that this territory would come to India only by international negotiations, not by any plebiscite.

At the time, out of regard for the sage, I took only a few people concerned into confidence concerning this conversation. I felt humble in the Master's presence, and came out dazed. There is no doubt that there was something in him which made my thoughts run to him time and again.

In December 1950, he died. I was the first to be told about it in Delhi on the telephone by our Consul-General. For two hours my mind went blank. I did not know why.

There was only a vague sense of being stunned. I did not feel like this even when Gandhiji, who was certainly very near to me, died; and I saw him dying. But after that, my mind went back to him again and again.

'AIM' Dec 1997, pages 4, 5, 6, 7, 8.

AN INTERVIEW WITH THE MOTHER

The Mother through her grace and love granted me an interview with her on the 29th May, 1954, and I passed some of my most precious moments of life with her.

I went to her with a number of questions in my mind, all of which I did not feel like putting before her, I wanted to ask her about the political, spiritual and cultural life in Africa, and how we, the Indians, should try to contribute to the growth of Africa, I had a mind to ask her, whether by the teaching of Sri Aurobindo not only Africa but the whole world can save itself. (from the great troubles that are looming large before them)

I narrated to the Mother the present political situation in East, Central and South Africa. There were the Mau Mau terrors in East Africa, the much opposed federation in Central Africa, and strong separatist apartheid move of Dr. Malan in South Africa, to all this the Mother simply said "They have their own way".

When I drew her attention to the big network of missionary's activities, she said "They are there to preach their own religion".

In reply to my question about the contribution by our Indians there, the Mother gave the very significant reply "Everything that India has to do here, they can do there" and added "You must know the Truth first"

And then I asked "What will be the position of Indians in Africa?" The Mother said "I don't know, it depends on the work they will do there" and she added "I have seen Durban, before Gandhi went there, there were some Indians living poorly, I don't know how it is now."

When I asked her about the spiritual possibilities in Africa, the Mother said "I don't know much about it, but at certain places our force is working."

Then I turned to my own questions I told her how a few years ago I had seen her in my dream, there I was lying at the feet of the Mother, and when my eyes met hers, I at once felt, that I had known her through the ages. And the Mother replied to this "Yes, it is a fact. You met me."

I told her about another dream of mine in which I saw books of Sri Aurobindo in some unknown parts of the world. To this the Mother said "Sri Aurobindo books are all over the world. Some people have also seen the photos of Sri Aurobindo in far off unexpected places."

I asked her how to change my outer nature, the Mother said "It's a very long business, you must know what you are doing at every moment" I marked that when the Mother was speaking her eyes were closed. She went on saying " You must have a steady will" and she told me at length about the development of the inner life.

I put her a question how to stop thoughts coming in during meditation, the Mother said ", as if speaking to a small child "Before you go to meditation, you must throw out all your thoughts."

Lastly I told her about Sri Aurobindo Library, in Livingstone. Before I finished my sentence, the Mother said "Yes, I know about it." Then I said, We are publishing pamphlets on every Darshan Day, and distributing them in various parts of Africa, we need your Blessing" The Mother said with her smile "Yes". She gave me flowers as a Blessing, and before taking her leave, I bowed at the feet, I really felt that they were the feet of the Divine Mother.

I turned up my eyes towards her face, and met her eyes straight, for the first time, alone, in my life. The Mother kept on looking at my eyes. It was a wonderful experience and I silently prayed to her "Make me live Divinely".

BHANABHAI PATEL

O divine Master, let Thy light fall into this chaos and bring forth from it a new world. Accomplish what is now in preparation and create a new humanity which may be the perfect expression of Thy new and sublime Law.

The Mother

Interview with The Mother

1. If you were asked to sum up, just in one sentence, your vision of India, what would be your answer?

India's true destiny is to be the Guru of the world.

2. Similarly, if you were asked to comment on the reality as you see it, how would you do so in one sentence?

The present reality is a big falsehood - hiding an eternal truth.

3. What, according to you, are the three main barriers that stand between the vision and the reality?

(a) Ignorance; (b) fear; (c) falsehood.

4. Are you satisfied with the over-all progress India has made since Independence?

No.

5. What is our most outstanding achievement in recent times? Why do you consider it so important?

Waking up of the yearning for Truth. Because without Truth there is no reality.

6. Likewise, can you name our saddest failure? On what grounds do you regard it as so tragic?

Insincerity. Because insincerity leads to ruin.

This is because the whole world is steeped in falsehood – so all actions that arise will be false, and this situation may continue for a long time and will bring much suffering to the people and the country.

The only thing to do is to pray – from the heart – for the Divine intervention as that is the only thing that can save us. And all people who can become conscious of this must decide very firmly to stand only on the Truth and to act only in the Truth. *There should be no compromise.* This is very essential. It is the only way.

Even if things seem to go wrong and badly for us, as indeed they will, because of the present prevailing falsehood - we should not be deterred from our own determination to stand on the Truth.

This is the only way.

O our Mother, O Soul of India.... Guide us so that the horizon of freedom opening before us may be also a horizon of true greatness and of thy true life in the community of the nations. Guide us so that we may be always on the side of great ideals and show to men thy true visage, as a leader in the ways of the spirit and a friend and helper of all the peoples.

'AIM' April 1996

Sri Aurobindo's Interview with Purani

I had an introduction to Shri V. V. S. Aiyar who was then staying at Pondicherry. It was in December 1918 that I arrived in Pondicherry. I did not stay long with Mr. Aiyar. I took up my bundle of books – mainly the *Arya* volumes – and went to 40, Rue François Martin, the *Arya* office, which was also Sri Aurobindo's residence. The house looked a little queer, – on the right, as one entered, were a few plantain trees and by its side a heap of broken tiles. On the left, at the edge of the open courtyard were seen four doors giving entrance to four rooms. The verandah outside was wide. It was about eight in the morning. The time for meeting Sri Aurobindo was fixed at three o'clock in the afternoon. I waited all the time in the house, occasionally chatting with the two inmates.who were there.

When I went up to meet him, Sri Aurobindo was sitting in a wooden chair behind a small table covered with an indigo blue cloth in the verandah upstairs. I felt a spiritual light surrounding his face. His look was penetrating. He knew me by my correspondence. I reminded him about my brother having met him at Baroda; he had not forgotten him. Then I informed him that our group was now ready to start revolutionary activity. It had taken us about eleven years to organise.

Sri Aurobindo remained silent for some time. Then he put me questions about my sadhana, spiritual practice. I described my efforts and added: "Sadhana is all right, – but it is difficult to concentrate on it so long as India is not free."

"Perhaps it may not be necessary to resort to revolutionary activity to free India," he said.

"But without that how is the British government to go from India?" I asked him.

"That is another question; but if India can be free without revolutionary activity, why should you execute the plan? It is better to concentrate on the yoga – spiritual development," he replied.

"But India is a land that has sadhana in its blood. When India is free, I believe thousands will devote themselves to yoga. But in the world of today who will listen to the truth or spirituality of slaves?" I asked him.

He replied: "India has already decided to win freedom and so there will certainly be found leaders and men to work for that goal. But all are not called to yoga. So, when you have the call, is it not better to concentrate upon it? If you want to carry out the revolutionary programme you are free to do it, but I cannot give my consent to it."

"But it was you who gave us the inspiration and the start for revolutionary activity. Why do you now refuse to give your consent to its execution?" I asked.

"Because I have done the work and I know its difficulties. Young men come forward to join the movement being inspired by idealism and enthusiasm. But these elements do not last long. It becomes very difficult to observe and exact discipline. Small groups begin to form within the organisation, rivalries grow between groups and even between individuals. There is competition for leadership. The agents of the government generally manage to join these organisations from the very beginning. And so they are unable to act effectively. Sometimes they sink so low as to quarrel even for money," he said calmly.

"But even supposing that I admit and agree to sadhana, that is, yoga, as being of greater importance and even intellectually understand that I should concentrate upon it, my difficulty is that I feel intensely that I must do something for the freedom of India. I have been unable to sleep soundly for the last two years and a half. I can remain quiet if I make a very strong effort. But the concentration of my whole being turns towards India's freedom. It is difficult for me to sleep till that is secured."

Sri Aurobindo remained silent for two or three minutes. It was a long pause. Then he said: "Suppose an assurance is given to you that India will be free?"

"Who can give such an assurance?" I could feel the echo of doubt and challenge in rny own question

Again he remained silent for three or four minutes. Then he looked at me and added: "Suppose I give you the assurance?"

I paused for half a minute, considered the question within myself and said: "If you give the assurance, I can accept it."

"Then, I give you the assurance that India will be free," he said in a serious tone.

My work was over, – the purpose of my visit to Pondicherry was served. My personal question and the problem of our group was solved! I then conveyed to him the message of Shri K. G. Deshpande from Baroda. I told him that financial help could be arranged from Baroda, if necessary, to which he replied, "At present what is required comes from Bengal, especially from Chandernagore. So, there is no need."

When the talk turned to Professor D. L. Purohit of Baroda, Sri Aurobindo recounted the incident of his visit to Pondicherry when he came here to inquire into the relation between the Church and the State. He paid a courtesy call to Sri Aurobindo as he knew him at Baroda. This resulted in his resignation from the Baroda state service on account of the pressure of the British Residency.

I conveyed to Sri Aurobindo the good news that after his resignation Mr. Purohit started practice as a lawyer and was quite successful, earning more than the pay he was getting as a professor. It was time for me to leave. The question of Indian freedom again arose in my mind, and at the time of taking leave, after I had got up to go, I could not repress the question – it was a question of life for me – "Are you quite sure that India will be free?"

I did not at that time realise the full import of my question. I wanted a guarantee, and though the assurance was given my doubts had not completely disappeared.

Sri Aurobindo became very serious. His gaze was fixed at the sky that appeared beyond the window. Then he looked at me and putting his fist on the table he said:

"You can take it from me, it is as certain as the rising of the sun tomorrow. The decree has already gone forth, it may not be long in coming."

I bowed down to him. That day in the train after nearly two years I was able at last to sleep soundly. In my mind was fixed for ever the picture of that scene: the two of us standing near the small table, my earnest question, that upward gaze, and that quiet and firm voice with the power in it to shake the world, that firm fist planted on the table – the symbol of self-confidence of the divine Truth. There may be rank Kaliyuga, the Iron Age, in the whole world but it is the great fortune of India that she has sons who know the Truth and have an unshakable faith in it, and can risk their lives for it. In this significant fact is contained the divine destiny of India and of the world.

After meeting Sri Aurobindo I was quite relieved of the great strain, I felt that Indian freedom was a certainty.

Sri Aurobindo Pages 293, 294, 295.

O Lord, Thou art our safeguard, our only happiness, Thou art our resplendent light, our pure love, our hope and our strength. Thou art our life, the reality of our being!

The Mother

The Mother's Interview with Purani

After seeing one or two institutions, we made for the parade ground. Mother came in tripping lightly from the tennis court dressed in the same manner as before, her blue-green scarf fluttering in the wind round her neck.

Then she went into a small office, where, a few minutes later, I was ushered in. She sat on a high-backed small chair, her feet on a footstool. Her eyes were transparent, almost clear as crystal.

I told her of my personal problems, of my old struggles, of Sri Aurobindo's message and the message of the Gangotri.

She replied in a quiet, firm tone, in a simple straightforward way. There was no attempt on her part to play the teacher or 'mystic or as someone of superior power.' "I heard of you from Sri Aurobindo," she said. "He also showed me one of your letters, that was," she tried to recollect, "in October 1950, if I remember rightly."

I had forgotten all about it. I had sent a letter to Sri Aurobindo through Jauhar. "He showed me your letter," Mother said, "and told me that he would not like to send any reply. But he added that you had possibilities and that one day you would find your soul." She paused.

"At that time", she continued, "he was very much exercised over the manifestation of wickedness all over the world; he concentrated all his power on bringing light into the world. When he left his body, it was glowing for days with the concentrated light of his spirit. You know how grand he looked. The body looked grander, after he had left it. There was no decomposition, but after some days the face showed signs of shrivelling up. His body was then buried."

And here she passed a finger over her left eyelid. It may have been an instinctive gesture, for her eyes were not wet and she spoke calmly, though with quiet emphasis as if Sri Aurobindo were still alive. "But he is still alive as living as ever," she resumed, "and will continue to live. We feel it every day. You told me that for many months he seemed to be haunting you. It is not only your experience, but of many."

I remained quiet; she continued: "We are determined – he and I – to complete what he lived for." She was silent for a little while and looked into space away from me, and then in a low voice said as if in reminiscence: "India must maintain the spiritual leadership of the world; if she does not, she will collapse, and with it will go the whole world."

"About yourself," she said, "he was very clear. You follow the lines of your own development and, as he said, you will gain your soul. As regards the message which you received, it is clear to me. You must devote yourself to proclaming your truth."

There was a little silence between us, a little tenseness in the atmosphere. Then I brought down the conversation to earth and asked her about the progress of the Sri Aurobindo University. "You have seen how we have begun," she said. "Why not invite a few professors to come and study Sri Aurobindo's philosophy and mysticism?" I asked. "I have been receiving letters from persons interested in his message, who want to come here," she replied. "I am receiving letters also from parents about sending their children. But I do not believe in starting in an ostentatious way. I am building up slowly, step by step, but firmly, and in ten years you will see what this university will be like." .

'The Life of Sri Aurobindo' – A.B. Purani.

The grace and protection are always with you. When in any inner or outer difficulty or trouble do not allow it to oppress you; take refuge with the Divine Force that protects.

If you do that always with faith and sincerity you will find something opening in you which will always remain calm and peaceful in spite of all superficial disturbances.

Sri Aurobindo

Sri Aurobindo's Interview with Dilipkumar Roy

Dilip: I have come to know... to ascertain rather... if I can be initiated... I mean I want to practice your yoga to start with, if possible.

Sri Aurobindo: You must tell me clearly what it is exactly that you seek, and why you want to do my yoga.

Dilip: Suppose I suggested – or rather suffer me to ask if you could help me in attaining or shall we say discovering, the object of life?.

Sri Aurobindo: That is not an easy question to answer, for I know of no one desideratum which is cherished equally by all, any more than I know of an object of life equally treasured by all. The object or aim of life cannot but vary with various people, and seekers, too, approach yoga with diverse aims. Some want to practise yoga to get away from life, like the (illusionist) mayavadi: these want to renounce life altogether, since, this phenomenal life, they contend, is an illusion, maya, which hides the ultimate reality. There are others who aspire after a supreme love or bliss. Yet others want from yoga power or knowledge or a tranquil poise impervious to the shocks of life. So you must first of all be definite as to what, precisely you seek in yoga.

Dilip: I want to know, if yoga could, in the last resort, lead to a solution of the anomalies of life with all its native sufferings and humiliations.

Sri Aurobindo: You mean transcendent knowledge?.

Dilip: If you like – but then no – for I want bliss too, crowning this wisdom.

Sri Aurobindo: You can certainly get either from yoga.

Dilip: May I then aspire to an initiation from you?

Sri Aurobindo: You may, provided you agree to its conditions and your call is strong.

Dilip: Couldn't you give me an idea about the nature of these conditions and about this call you speak of. Sri Aurobindo: May I ask what you mean exactly?

Dilip: I gathered from your booklet Yogic Sadhan, that you called yourself, a Trantrik who believed in lila, and not a follower of Shankara believing in maya. You have written for instance: 'To fulfil God in life is man's manhood' and if my memory doesn't fail me, you said in your Life Divine: 'We must accept the many-sidedness of the Manifestation even while we assert the unity of the manifested.

Sri Aurobindo: It is true that I am a believer in lila. But why exactly do you refer to that?.

Dilip: I wanted to make sure whether you really meant what you wrote in your Yogic Sadhan. I hope, too, that your yoga doesn't make it binding on one to live

like a cave dweller who disowns the many-mooded, active life or, shall we say,
like a passive pensioner whose day is done? This hope, happily, has been fostered
by your repudiation of mayavada.

Sri Aurobindo: I see what you mean, well, yes, I am not a mayavadi, happily, for you as well as for me. But, incidentally, I am the author of book Yogic Sadhan.

Dilip: How do you mean?

Sri Aurobindo: Haven't you heard of automatic writing?

Dilip: Planchette?

Sri Aurobindo: Not exactly. I merely held the pen while a disembodied being wrote off what he wished, using my pen and hand.

Dilip: May I ask why you lent yourself to such writing? ("At the time I was
trying to find out how much of truth and how much of subliminal suggestion from
the submerged consciousness there might be in phenomena of this kind")

Sri Aurobindo: But let that pass. To return to your main question. You asked about the active life. Well, it isn't binding on you to renounce all that you value in your active life. What you must be ready to renounce is attachment to everything on that plane whether you live within or outside the wheel of karma, action. For if you keep these attachments, the Light from above will not be able to work unhampered to effect the radical transformation of your nature.

Dilip: Does that imply that I must forego, say, all human sympathy and true
friendship, all joy of life and fellow feeling?

Sri Aurobindo: It doesn't.

'Among the Great' pages 205 to 207

Dilip: But must I necessarily be called upon to forego – everything?

Sri Aurobindo: "You may not be – outwardly, that is," he said. "But that won't make any very material difference, since your inner attitude has to be that of complete freedom all the same – the ideal must be *nirliptata*, non-attachment. If you can be truly non-attached within, you need not have to tear off the outward strappings of bondage. But remember that you must always be ready to shove aside anything that is incompatible with yoga, for that surely is one of its major conditions.

Dillip: Does that apply to things that do not, properly speaking, belong to the
material plane, say music which I love so dearly? Must I renounce that too?

Sri Aurobindo: "I haven't said you *must*," he smiled again indulgently, "only, if yoga were the central thing in your life you would not be so nervous at the prospect of having to give up music for its sake, would you?"

I hung my head discountenanced.

Dilip: "I would not have you infer," I pleaded, "that I couldn't possibly give up music. Only I am not yet persuaded that yoga will make it up to me. My problem may be somewhat naive but it is a problem none the less. It is like this: I don't find it hard to give up a lower thing for a higher one provided I have some foretaste of the latter. But so long as I have no clear idea of what yoga has to give, why must I gamble away the tangible for the elusive? Before I burn my boats can't I legitimately claim even a glimpse of what the deep has in store for me?.

Sri Aurobindo: Didn't I tell you just now that you need not necessarily give up your music or something just as tangible for that matter what is obligatory is that should any activity or idea or habit or attachment or preconception prove an impediment on the way, you have to discard it when so required.

Dilip: "But you haven't answered my question about the compensation. Or perhaps it is taboo to have such an intellectual curiosity or scepticism, if you will?"

Sri Aurobindo: "Not quite, only yoga, you must know, is not a matter of intellectual appraisement or recognition: it is essentially a matter of realization through self-dedication. As for your other question, surely the compensations of yoga are deep as well as abiding. Only, you can't summon them to prove their validity before your mental dock. But let me tell you here that your difficulties aren't what you presume them to be: I mean they are not mental at bottom. The truth of the matter is this: so long as the joys which belong to the lower planes continue to be too vividly real and covetable you will find ready enough reasons why you shouldn't decline them. You can forego them only when you have had a call of the higher joys, when the lower ones begin to pall, sound hollow. The Promised Land of the Spirit begins from the frontier of worldly enjoyments, to start with."

"But why is it," I asked after a pause, "that one can't expect to have even a glimpse beforehand of this Land? Because of the thick walls of our worldly desires?"

Sri Aurobindo: "Your premise here is not quite correct," he objected. "For even when we live in the world of these desires the glimpse, the call, comes to us through chinks and rifts of dissatisfaction and surfeit. Only, it doesn't last long until you are somewhat purified, for then only do you really begin to be open to it. The darkness returns intermittently after the light because it takes long to get our whole being open to the light. That is why yoga pushes us urgently upwards to altitudes where the light can be shut out no more by clouds. And it is just because yoga is such an ascent, of consciousness, that any attachment to or desire for lures and prizes on the lower planes, material, intellectual or aesthetic, must eventually prove a shackle."

'Among the Great' pages 212 - 213

QUESTIONS AND ANSWERS

If you were asked to sum up, just in one sentence, your vision of India, what would be your answer?

India's true destiny is to be the Guru of the world.

Similarly, if you were asked to comment on the reality as you see it, how would you do so in one sentence?

The present reality is a big falsehood hiding an eternal truth.

What, according to you, are the three main barriers that stand between the vision and the reality?

Ignorance; (b) Fear; (c) Falsehood.

Are you satisfied with the overall progress India has made since Independence?

No.

What is our most outstanding achievement in recent times? Why do you consider it so important?

Waking up of the yearning for Truth. Because without Truth there is no reality.

Likewise, can you name our saddest failure? On what grounds do you regard it as so tragic?

Insincerity. Because insincerity leads to ruin.

26.10.1964

What is the duty of every Indian today in the present emergency?

Overgrow your small egoistic personality and become a worthy child of our Mother India, fulfil your duties with honesty and rectitude, and always keep cheerful and confident with a steady trust in the Divine's Grace.

January, 1965

In view of the present and the future of national and international living, what is it that India should aim at in education?

Prepare her children for the rejection of falsehood and the manifestation of Truth.

By what steps could the country proceed to realise this high aim ? How can a beginning in that direction be?

Make matter ready to manifest the Spirit.

What is India's true genius and what is her destiny?

49

To teach to the world that matter is false and impotent unless it becomes the manifestation of the Spirit.

How does the Mother view the progress of Science and Technology in India? What contribution can they make to the growth of the Spirit in man?

Its only use is to make the material basis stronger, completer and more effective for the manifestation of the Spirit.

The country feels much concerned about national unity. What is the Mother's vision of things? How will India do her duty by herself and by the world?

The unity of all the nations is the compelling future of the world. But for the unity of all nations to be possible, each nation must first realise its own unity.

The language problem harasses India a good deal. What would be our correct attitude in this matter?

Unity must be a living fact and not the imposition of an arbitrary rule. When India will be one, she will have spontaneously a language understood by all.

Education has normally become literacy and a social status. Is it not an unhealthy trend? But how to give to education its inner worth and intrinsic enjoyability?

Get out of conventions and insist on the growth of the soul.

What illusions and delusions our education is today beset with? How could we possibly keep clear of them?

The almost exclusive importance given to success, career and money.

Insist on the paramount importance of the contact with the Spirit and the growth and manifestation of the Truth of the being.

05.08.1965

How to find back India's soul ?

Become conscious of your psychic being. Let your psychic being become intensely interested in India's Soul and aspire towards it, with an attitude of service; and if you are sincere you will succeed.

15.06.1970

Diary 2000

Udar Pinto's Visit to Savitri Bhavan

How will Sri Aurobindo and the Mother come back?

I asked the Mother one day, "Mother, how will Sri Aurobindo come back? Will he be born?" Because I can't imagine Sri Aurobindo coming as a baby, I told Mother. She said, "No Udar, he will not be born, he will not come as a baby. He will come ready-made, projected into the world." Ready-made: that is, a complete being, that will remain like that: it will not grow older, it will remain constantly the same being. And in *Savitri* come these lines, in the canto called "The House of the Spirit and the New Creation":

> In these new worlds projected he became
> A portion of the universal gaze,
> A station of the all-inhabiting light,
> A ripple on a single sea of peace.   *(p. 325)*

So in *Savitri* itself it is confirmed that Sri Aurobindo will come back in quite a different way, what Mother called "the supramental way". And Mother herself said, "If I leave my body, I will also come back in a supramental way." And that is given in a passage that comes later:

> *A seed shall be sown in Death's tremendous hour,*
> *A branch of heaven transplant to human soil;*
> *Nature shall overleap her mortal step;*
> *Fate shall be changed by an unchanging will.*   *(p. 346)*

Sri Aurobindo's yoga

There is another passage that I would like to recite, because Mother told me that Sri Aurobindo was not born an avatar, he became an avatar. Some avatars were born, and some became. Jesus Christ and Krishna were born avatars. Buddha and others became avatars. And Mother said that becoming an avatar is a very very tremendous physical strain. She said it is impossible for us to realise how much Sri Aurobindo suffered physically, to pass through that stage. He had to overcome all the recalcitrant parts of our being and go beyond. And he writes of "anguish":

> *In anguish we labour that from us may rise*
> *A larger-seeing man with nobler heart,*
> *A golden vessel of the incarnate Truth,*
> *The executor of the divine attempt*
> *Equipped to wear the earthly body of God,*
> *Communicant and prophet and lover and king.*   *(p. 342)*

Sri Aurobindo went through all of the Raja Yoga, and came to the final goal of all yoga. The final goal of yoga is what they call *moksha*. Moksha is when you realise the self of your own being, and you realise that that self and the Divine are the same, so that there is merging, a union of the Divine and the self. And that is the end of all endeavour. Once you come to God, you don't need to go any further. And up to now this has been the goal of all spiritual effort, I would even say all true religion has the goal of going to God. And once you reach God. you don't need anything else. Up to now that has been the accepted goal. Now, for the first time in the history of the world, somebody has said it is not enough – and that is Sri Aurobindo. It is not enough to go to God. We must bring God down here on this earth and make him work here, not just in heaven! This is Sri Aurobindo, and this is what I like about him. I find this wonderful. We must find God and make him work here, not go off into some heaven. He calls that an escape. Here are the lines:

> *O soul, it is too early to rejoice!*
> *Thou hast reached the boundless silence of the Self,*
> *Thou has leaped into a glad divine abyss;*
> *But where hast thou thrown Self's mission and Self's power?*
> *On what dead bank on the Eternal's road?*
> *One was within thee who was self and world,*
> *What hast thou done for his purpose in the stars?*
> *Escape brings not the victory and the crown!*
> *Something thou cam'st to do from the Unknown,*
> *But nothing is finished and the world goes on*
> *Because only half God's cosmic work is done*
> *Only the everlasting No has neared*
> *And stared into thy eyes and killed thy heart:*
> *But where is the Lover's everlasting Yes,*
> *And immortality in the secret heart,*
> *The voice that chants to the creator Fire,*
> *The symbolled Om, the great assenting Word,*
> *The bridge between the rapture and the calm,*
> *The passion and the beauty of the Bride,*
> *The chamber where the glorious enemies kiss,*
> *The smile that saves, the golden peak of things?*
> *This too is Truth at the mystic fount of Life.*
> *A black veil has been lifted; we have seen*
> *The mighty shadow of the omniscient Lord,*
> *But who has lifted up the veil of light*
> *And who has seen the body of the King?*   (p.310-311)

This is what he wants, the body of the King.

As I say, this is the first time in the history of the world that somebody has said that going to God is not enough. And for this reason you must understand that this is a yoga that is not at all like other yogas. Many people, even in the Ashram, don't realise that. They think that Sri Aurobindo is a great yogi, a maharishi, and they come to him for blessings and all that. But you can go to so many yogis and get blessings from them – Sri Aurobindo is something completely different.

So Sri Aurobindo is doing his yoga. The Divine Mother addresses him as "Son of Strength".

> *"O Son of Strength who climbst creation's peaks,*
> *No soul is thy companion in the light;*
> *Alone thou standest at the eternal doors.*
> *What thou hast won is shine, but ask no more.*
> *O Spirit aspiring in an ignorant frame,*
> *O Voice arisen from the Inconscient's world,*
> *How shalt thou speak for men whose hearts are dumb,*
> *Make purblind earth the soul's seer-vision's home*
> *Or lighten the mystery of the senseless globe?*
> *I am the Mystery beyond reach of mind,*
> *I am the goal of the travail of the suns;*
> *My fire and sweetness are the cause of life.*
> *But too immense my danger and my joy.*
> *Awake not the immeasurable descent,*
> *Speak not my secret name to hostile time;*
> *Man is too weak to bear the Infinite's weight.*
> *Truth born too soon might break the imperfect earth.*
> *Leave the all-seeing Power to hew its way:*
> *In thy single vast achievement reign apart*
> *Helping the world with thy great lonely days.*   *(p. 335j*

This 'great lonely days' is something that touches me very well, because as I told you, I used to be working in Sri Aurobindo's room, and I would see him ... of course sometimes he would be dictating Savitri, but at other times he would be just sitting there looking into eternity, just like that. And these words, 'great lonely days' bring back to me the picture of Sri Aurobindo just sitting and looking, not a word, not a movement - a wonderful sight.

And there is another line in *Savitri:*

> *Lonely his days and splendid like the sun's.*   *(p. 45)*

That is the picture of Sri Aurobindo to me.

How did man come on Earth?

Now we come to the question of how Man came to the earth. Of course the scientists say that man evolved out of the ape. Sri Aurobindo does not accept that. The ape certainly went to a certain extent, but there was not a change from ape to man. Man came completely differently. He describes it here:

> *A lightning from the heights that think and plan,*
> *Ploughing the air of life with vanishing trails,*
> *Man, sole awake in an unconscious world,*
> *Aspires in vain to change the cosmic dream.*
> *Arrived from some half-luminous Beyond*
> *He is a stranger in the mindless vasts;*
> *A traveller in his oft-shifting home*
> *Amid the tread of many infinities,*
> *He has pitched a tent of life in desert Space.*
> *Heaven's fixed regard beholds him from above,*
> *In the house of Nature a perturbing guest,*
> *A voyager twixt Thought's inconstant shores,*
> *A hunter of unknown and beautiful Powers,*
> *A nomad of the far mysterious Light,*
> *In the wide ways a little spark of God. (p. 336)*

That is man. He has not come from the apes. So there are things like that, that must be understood, and all these things are given in *Savitri*.

> *My light shall be in thee, my strength thy force.*
> *Let not the impatient Titan drive thy heart,*
> *Ask not the imperfect fruit, the partial prize.*
> *Only one boon, to greaten thy spirit, demand;*
> *Only one joy, to raise thy kind, desire.*
> *Above blind fate and the antagonist powers*
> *Moveless there stands a high unchanging Will;*
> *To its omnipotence leave thy work's result.*
> *All things shall change in God's transfiguring hour.* (p. 340-341)

Now here there is one very important line that I want you to note:

Only one boon, to greaten thy spirit, demand.

The Mother told me, "People come and ask me for blessings, for so many things, they want to pass their examinations, they want to get a job, they're going on a journey, this thing, that thing, for so many things they come and ask my blessings – I give blessings, but for only one thing: that is, the growth of the spirit." To greaten the spirit – this is the only boon we should demand. She said: "That's the only thing that interests me in anybody – the growth of the spirit." And she said, "Sometimes it's a bit dangerous to ask blessings for a marriage." She said, "Sometimes my blessings can break up a marriage, so be careful when you ask me for blessings for marriages." Mother had quite a good sense of humour you know – both Sri Aurobindo and the Mother.

What we need

The next thing I'll tell you about: Sri Aurobindo makes a complaint to the Divine:

"How shall I rest content with mortal days
And the dull measure of terrestrial things,
I who have seen behind the cosmic mask
The glory and the beauty of thy face?
Hard is the doom to which thou bindst thy sons!
How long shall our spirits battle with the Night
And bear defeat and the brute yoke of Death,
We who are vessels of a deathless Force

Source: Invocation August 1999

55

MODERN REVIEW, VOL. XLIV, NO 1: JULY 1928

India Will Speak Through Your Voice

RABINDRANATH TAGORE
(Nobel Laureate, India)

At the very first sight I could realise that he (Sri Aurobindo) had been seeking for the soul and had gained it, and through this long process of realisation had accumulated within him a silent power of inspiration. His face was radiant with an inner light and his serene presence made it evident to me that his soul was not crippled and cramped to the measure of some tyrannical doctrine, which takes delight in inflicting wounds upon life ...

I felt that the utterance of the ancient Hindu Rishi spoke from him of that equanimity which gives the human soul its freedom of entrance into the All. I said to him, 'You have the Word and we are waiting to accept it from you. India will speak through your voice to the world, "Hearken to me".'...

Years ago I saw Aurobindo in the atmosphere of his earlier heroic youth and I sang to him,

'Aurobindo, accept the salutation from Rabindranath.'[1]

Today[2] I saw him in a deeper atmosphere of a reticent richness of wisdom and again sang to him in silence,

'Aurobindo, accept the salutation from Rabindranath.'

---

[1] A line from the poem "Salutation" by Tagore, published in 1907. The original in Bengali is translated into English by Kshitish Chandra Sen, see *Sri Aurobindo Mandir Annual,* 1944, pp. 2-3.

[2] Rabindranath Tagore met Sri Aurobindo at Pondicherry on 29.5.1928; after 21 years.

'AIM' Dec. 1997

SOUND—AN UNPUBLISHED INTERVIEW

I MEDITATED at the Mother's feet for a while, then looked up.

"Your song on 'Sound'* last evening," she said, "was power, power, power – all through. You expressed all the conflicts of Nature so powerfully and truly that I was very pleased. I saw descending upon you from above an intense white light and a great power. Under its pressure there was proceeding from you a very generous distribution of vital force – in the best sense of the term – all around you. And the resolution of the conflicts into the chords of Victory was remarkable. Even, above some of the notes you sang I contacted a vast Peace and Ananda, which will be expressed completely and permanently all through when you will be identified with it. But even at this stage of your sadhana the peace that was waiting above lasted for not an inconsiderable space of time; and in some portions of your music I saw you were not you but Music itself."

"That's what constitutes genius," the Mother added with one of her-sweetest smiles. "Of course you know I don't believe in complimenting, and I don't say all this to you to pay you compliments. I tell you this because I saw it."

"And this source of Peace and Ananda that you contacted at times," continued the Mother, "I wanted to bring down. But as you haven't yet experienced it, it didn't come down to stay, or rather, it didn't last. Nevertheless, the notes you sang on Peace rang, at times, with an intensely concentrated fervour. Your theme of Sound was truly expressed. The conclusion towards which it was leading was the grandeur of the descent into this world of a greater World beyond, and that reminded me of Beethoven's grand Ninth Symphony. You have heard it, haven't you?"

"I have, Mother," I said "it is wonderful".

"Your music yesterday seemed to me to be making an opening towards that grand power, of course, not in the European way, but in the Indian way – and not yet in its native fullness and glory but in the full process of formation and crystallisation."

"Great geniuses, when they truly achieve great things," the Mother went on, "lose the sense of their separate ego and identity – *namarupa* – and become the thing itself, the thing they manifest; it was so with you when you sang certain of these notes, which were truly marvellous. These could not come down to stay, to endure, at this stage of your sadhana, but when you'll have had experience of the Divine – this will be permanent, it is then you will touch the acme of your personality. It is not yet come, but it is fast coming. And the white light descending

---

* "Your song Nada (Sound) is truly wonderful. And it is a beautiful poem, too, not colourless and poetically wooden like Satyen Datta's lines in his Bengali reproduction of Mandakranta. As for the inner rhythm, it is surely the Mandakranta Rhythm, less elegiac than the movement of the Meghaduta, but still the same. Your statement of the distinction — in the spirit of the movement as opposed to its body, or rather an immobile clay figure representing the mobile body (for that is what Satyen Datta's reproduction comes to)–is, I believe, quite accurate."   Sri Aurobindo

on you which was also flowing and reaching others was dazzling like, what shall I say – you have seen snowy mountain-tops reflecting dazzling white light, haven't you?"

"Yes, Mother," I said in great joy.

"The light I saw round you was like that," the Mother said, "It was a descent of Power—Power—Power concentrated."

"It is so pleasing to me," Mother went on, "to see true and rapid growth in people, to see them expanding and rising to heights, to rise and swell and grow – in every possible direction."

"But how about being ambitious, Mother?" I asked. "For sometimes I feel I am so irretrievably ambitious by nature..."

"I always blame people for not being ambitious enough," countered the Mother. "I always tell people – 'Be more ambitious – ambitious to grow, ambitious to become a divine warrior, ambitious to achieve things really worthwhile.' The only thing is, the human limitations must be consciously transcended. Otherwise unimpeded true growth is not possible."

"I have lately had some inexplicably and, if I may say so, curiously vivid feelings, Mother," I said, "I have felt again and again that I must grow and grow as I have never done before, only I must purge myself of all personal ambition and that ruthlessly. My one-pointed aim and endeavour must be, this voice has persistently cried out to me, to dedicate all my gifts for Divine Service. And even in my most trying moments in the course of my sadhana, I have never for a moment felt tempted to exploit my capacities for purely personal ends as used to be my wont before. My greatest defect in this connection seems to me to be that I am still extremely sensitive to praise even of outsiders and charlatans even, which praise fortunately for me, however, comes my way but rarely, now-a-days – covered as I have become with infamy—as you know."

"What need have you for the appreciation of outsiders, whether competents or charlatans, since *you* know you have come for the Divine sincerely, and that the Divine has accepted you? Let the whole world misunderstand you, how can it make even a little difference now? – But you need not look frightfully abashed, Dilip," added the Mother twinkling at me, patting me on the hand, "few artists are there who aren't avid of praise, who don't feel morally convinced that the world has been created to circle round them, and if far more serious defects of your character have had their backs so thoroughly broken, this pertinacious enemy will too certainly be prevailed upon to capitulate, don't you worry. As for your difficulties too, they will disappear as shamefacedly as one could wish. This, incidentally, I saw once again yesterday as you were singing. For as I told you just now, yesterday, while you were producing certain specific notes, I saw you no longer as Dilip, but as Music pure: then it was that flashed before me your true being (which, by the way, is an old acquaintance of mine), a splendid being. But about this I don't wish to speak *now*. You will yourself know later on."*

* As reported by the author in his language.

The Mother changed the topic and added: "Most people are content with what they are – that is to say, with their human mould and limitations, talking a lot of nonsense about 'being oneself'. But it is only when they realise the Divine that they are face to face with their real selves. We get a partial glimpse of this truth when we see the geniuses working miracles. They achieve the impossible – how?– simply by ceasing to be themselves, transcending their mundane moulds and becoming identified more or less with what they express, embody."

"When you were singing yesterday," the Mother continued, "you testified to this once again, when you were no longer yourself, I said 'but become identified with what you expressed, or rather, with what got expressed through you.' "

I hung on every word that dropped from the Mother's lips, overjoyed. For the Mother had seldom spoken to me like this.

"It is very remarkable and interesting," pursued the Mother, "to trace the changes and evolution in your music and creative power. The fund of vital force in you one day suddenly turned and from that day forth your music was fundamentally altered in its character and outlook; you have continued ever since progressively to succeed in expressing what you sang. For instance when you sang your song on Kali the other day, she had actually appeared in the subtle and danced before my eyes, as I had told you, and also the red colour had appeared. When you sang of Krishna, the deep blue colour – which is his colour – had appeared, and just when I invoked him and he was about to respond you stopped."

"I regret it so much, the Mother," I said smiling, "I wish I had known."

"No matter," said the Mother, smiling, "it will come back later, all in good time. Besides, Krishna is difficult to invoke in this way,– much more difficult than Kali... But what I was emphasising was that you have been succeeding more and more in expressing your theme: the white light which developed yesterday is too an instance in point."

"I see a most beautiful shimmering golden colour on your face, Mother," I exclaimed, in great joy, "this morning I saw too, a most lovely green on the wall – most like a lambent flame. But I have never before seen this sort of flashing gold on your face at such close quarters. What does it mean?"

"It shows that your inner vision is developing," said the Mother with a beaming smile, "and when this power will grow further a new and vivid world will open before your eyes. This is only the beginning, the outer fringe, as Sri Aurobindo wrote to you the other day when you started seeing these colours everywhere round about you, which he advised you to develop."*

* "Develop this power of that inner sense and all that it brings you," wrote Sri Aurobindo, in Feb. 1932. "These first seeings are only an outer fringe – behind lie whole worlds of experience which fill what seems to the natural man the gap (your Russel's 'inner void') between the earth consciousness and the Eternal and Infinite."

N.B.: Sri Aurobindo wrote to Sahana Devi on her singing of this evening: "Your singing was wonderful today; your voice has marvellously improved; it had a warmth and richness and variety and power of expression you never showed before."   10.7.32.

59

"If you had more of these powers of vision," the Mother added, "you would have been delighted to see – what I saw the other day while meditating with you – how beautifully certain lovely colours were organising themselves within you; symbolical of the flowering of your creative powers.... It is also so very interesting to me to observe how the musical atmosphere is gradually concentrating round all the participants – to notice how the first amateurish feeling of the sadhikas too are vanishing."

"And I wanted it to be precisely like that, as you know," the Mother went on. "I want people to come and hear such music here the like of which they can hear nowhere else. I don't care to have music here to please a few people who have nothing to do or who are easily satisfied.'.'

"With your blessings, Mother, it will be like that I am sure," I said, "and one of the reasons is that I do feel the bubbling of such a new power when I sing now-a-days and such new turns of melodies when I compose that I feel convinced thanks to your grace."

"I want to tell you, Mother, of two very significant dreams I have had of late," I added after a pause, "One was day before yesterday: I dreamt first that I was questioning myself: What will be your relationship with others after the Realisation? To this the answer came: you will have a new relationship which will be determined by a common seeking – the quest of the Divine."

"It is not a dream – it is an experience, for the answer is precise and correct," said the Mother, pleased.

"I knew it to be so at once, Mother," I said overjoyed, "for as soon as I heard this voice I felt such a fervour of devotion that I woke up in joy."

"I regard this as particularly significant in as much as I have often caught myself wondering how I would react to the friendly approaches of my former friends," I added, "as also because the problems of friendship have appeared a little difficult – always. What about the intimacies of my many friends to which I used once to respond vividly and on which I still lovingly dwell?– I have often asked myself. To all these questionings this voice gave a reply which, curiously, gave me deep peace – not that the answer was in any way remarkably striking or new or original – but that it came home to me with a curious and altogether new force – like a force of realisation, almost."

"I have told you before that such dreams are symbolical of realisation," the Mother said. "And what is the other?"

"I saw as though I was sailing on board a boat bound for Europe," I said, "where applause and reception were awaiting me. I suppose I saw this because I have of late received some interesting and glowing accounts from my friends Udaysankar and Timirbaran to which I have given some publicity in the Press, congratulating them on their getting on so famously in Europe, which work I once deeply valued. It gave me a sort of wish-fulfilment too, maybe, for I must own I have, sometimes, felt a short-lived stir within me – particularly on receipt of some letters from Europe wishing me to come to Europe on a lecture tour – for which I do feel a little ashamed. But let that pass. To come back to the dream:

"It was a most cogent sort of dream, Mother," I continued, "for at first I found a sort of ticklish sensation on the neck. But as soon as the boat weighed anchor, I felt a deep melancholy – a sense of utter futility – an indefinable poignant nostalgia for something precious and beyond my reach. By the time the steamer touched the next harbour my anguish had become all but unbearable, when something very remarkable happened:

"I ruminated on the successes of all such vain egoistic missions and a deep dissatisfaction seized hold of me: I lost faith in my so-called self-imposed mission, and began asking myself the wherefore of it all: Why must I sweat thus – as I used to, once – for fame and name and art and so forth? To what end? Why even move heaven and earth to convince Europe that Indian music is great? Why such a tremendous expenditure of my precious energy to compass something which leaves the eternal hunger of the heart unappeased?– Why–why–why?– surged up all around me, when suddenly your image, Mother, flashed – with that of Sri Aurobindo, and I heard a voice within me saying: There – there you must go, your life's work awaits you there and not in the garish unreality of such transitory applause and volatile self-satisfaction. For what use is it all if the Divine remains veiled – unrealised? What use is your ambition if it is not directed towards the Divine Realisation?– And I found the key to my misery, Mother, and I left the ship for refuge at your feet. Does it not show how much I have changed in the last few years?"

"It does of course," replied the Mother, pleased. "And as for your questioning about ambition, too, it was quite right. I have told you that ambition in itself isn't a bad thing at all. Only it must be well-directed. Let it be your ambition to be content with nothing but the highest."

DILIP KUMAR ROY

(Revised and approved and slightly altered by Sri Aurobindo on 11.7.32)

SOUND

WHO is she, the Formless, flaming and hurtling through
the sky in the flashes of the lightning?
Who is she, the Fearless, clanging in the breath of the
storm-wind and the music of the tempest?
Who is there dancing sombre in the roar and the
swaying orgies of the ocean?
Who is there resonant in the ululation on high
and monster drum-beats of the thunder?
Who is the ravishing one that comes pouring as rain
in a melodious murmur and patter?—
Like unto a Mother of Peace responding to the child-soul

'Mother India' August 2000, pages 603-607

61

A Conversation with the Mother

Mother: Is it January?
Yes, Mother – it is January.
Read what is written here.
(Every month I used to take to Mother a large calendar on which flowers were painted and on which She used to write a prayer)
"In this year of Sri Aurobindo's centenary, let us strive to be worthy of Him..."
And then?
"...by following His teaching faithfully in order to prepare the advent of the superman. Happy New Year."
What flower is this? *(pointing to the painted flower)*
"Superhumanity".
Eh?
This is "superhumanity". The name of this flower is "superhumanity".
Which flower is it?
This flower – it is the dahlia.
Dahlia! Yes, yes.
(Mother writes the following prayer for the month of February and draws "OM" underneath)
"Nature rediscovers the Divine in a blissful surrender."

With the help of OM one can realise the Divine. OM has a transforming power. OM represents the Divine.
Yes, it represents the Divine. It represents the Divine.
OM, but OM is the sound?
The sound – They say that all the aspirations of the world when going towards the Divine make O----M, like that. *(Mother chants the word)*
Yes, Mother.
And then, that is why they say "OM".
Mother, please say it once again. Please say it again.
Eh?
OM, it is fine, Mother, it was very beautiful. (Mother laughs) Mother, once more, please.
O----M.
And now?
It is like this everywhere. O----M. O----M.
Yes, Mother.
Look here, I was in France some, I think, 60 years ago. There was a Frenchman who came back from the Himalayas, who had stayed there some time and he gave a lecture, and I listened to the lecture and in the lecture he said that when he was deep in the Himalayas, there was a Sannyasin whom he didn't know, came to see him and told him only this O----M and that he was completely changed. And then, when he said O----M, I felt the same change in me, ... as if the Divine was coming in. O----M. There you are. Good, good. Keep the secret.
Yes, Mother.
You will recall this: O----M. O----M. That's all. O----M. It must be manifested. If anything goes wrong, repeat OM, all will go well.

(Conversation of Mona Sarkar with the Mother in Jan. 1972, recorded by him from memory.)

SECTION III

Conversations

Invoking the Grace

Q: Does the intervention of the Grace come through a call?

When one calls? I think so. Anyway, not exclusively and solely. But certainly, yes, if one has faith in the Grace and an aspiration and if one does what a little child would when it runs to its mother and says: "Mamma, give me this", if one calls with that simplicity, if one turns to the Grace and says "Give me this", I believe it listens. Unless one asks for something that is not good for one, then it does not listen. If one asks from it something that does harm or is not favourable, it does not listen.

Q: What is the cause of this effect? Of the call?

Perhaps one was destined to call. That is: Did the hen produce the egg or the egg the hen? I don't know whether it is the Grace which makes you call the Grace or whether because the Grace is called the Grace comes. It is difficult to say.

Essentially, it is quite possible that what is most lacking is faith. There is always a tiny corner in the thought which doubts and debates. So that spoils everything. It is only just when one is in an absolutely critical situation, when the mind realises that it can do nothing, absolutely nothing, when it stands there quite stupid and incapable, then, at that moment, if one aspires for a higher help, the aspiration has exactly that kind of intensity which comes from despair, and that takes effect. But if your thought continues to argue, if it says: "Yes, yes, I have aspired, I have prayed, but God knows if this is the moment, and whether it will come and whether it is possible", well, then it is finished, it doesn't work.

... if one has trust in the divine Grace, if one has the faith that there is something in the world like the divine Grace, and that this something can answer a prayer, an aspiration, an invocation, then, after making one's mental formation, if one offers it to the Grace and puts one's trust in it, asks it to intervene and has the faith that it will intervene, then indeed one has a chance of success.

Try, and you will surely see the result.

Q: But, Mother, when one prays sincerely for the intervention of the Grace, doesn't one expect a particular result?

Excuse me, that depends on the tenor of the prayer. If one simply invokes the Grace or the Divine, and puts oneself in His hands, one does not expect a particular result. To expect a particular result one must formulate one's prayer, must ask for something. If you have only a great aspiration for the divine Grace and evoke it, implore it, without asking it for anything precise, it.is the Grace which will choose what it will do for you, not you.

Q: That is better, isn't it?

Ah! that's quite another question.

Why, it is higher in its quality, perhaps. But still, if one wants something precise, it is better to formulate it. If one has a special reason for invoking the Grace, it is better to formulate it precisely and clearly.

Of course, if one is in a state of complete surrender and gives oneself entirely, if one simply offers oneself to the Grace and lets it do what it likes, that is very good. But after that one must not question what it does! One must not say to it, "Oh! I did that with the idea of having this", for if one really has the idea of obtaining something, it is better to formulate it in all sincerity, simply, just as one sees it. Afterwards, it is for the Grace to choose if it will do it or not; but in any case, one will have formulated clearly what one wanted. And there is no harm in that.

Where it becomes bad is when the request is not granted and one revolts. Then naturally it becomes bad. It is at that moment one must understand that the desire one has, or the aspiration, may not have been very enlightened and that perhaps one has asked for something which was not exactly what was good for one. Then at that moment one must be wise and say simply, "Well, let Thy Will be done." But so long as one has an inner perception and an inner preference, there is no harm in formulating it. It is a very natural movement.

For example, if one has been foolish or has made a mistake and one truly, sincerely wishes never to do it again, well, I don't see any harm in asking for it. And in fact, if one asks for it with sincerity, a true inner sincerity, there is a great chance that it will be granted.

You must not think that the Divine likes to contradict you. He is not at all keen on doing it! He can see better than you what is really good for you; but it is only when it is absolutely indispensable that He opposes your aspiration. Otherwise He is always ready to give what you ask.

THE MOTHER
'AIM', April 1988, pages 13-15

Humanity

Q: How can humanity become one?

By becoming conscious of its origin.

*Q: What is the way of making the conciousness of
human unity grow in man?*

Spiritual education, that is to say an education which gives more
importance to the growth of the spirit than to any religious or moral
teaching or to the material so-called knowledge.

*

It is not through uniformity that you obtain unity...
   The true, the supreme Unity expresses itself in diversity. It is
mental logic that demands sameness.

'AIM' April 1996, page 34

* * * * *

QUESTIONS & ANSWERS

Answers From the Mother

*To a Frenchwoman who came to live at the
Sri Aurobindo Ashram in 1937, at the age of sixty-six.*

Nothing is inevitable. At every moment an intervention may come from a higher
plane into the material one and alter the course of circumstances. But in this
particular case there is a conflict between a very powerful mental construction
founded on medical opinion and your faith in the divine Grace.
   The power of this medical suggestion lies in the fact that it insinuates itself into
the subconscious and acts on the body from there, undetected even by the
conscious mind unless it is in the habit of scouring the subconscious with the vig-
ilance of a detective.
   So there we are – I cannot promise you that your faith in the Grace will be
intense and unshakable enough to overcome the harmful effect of these medical
suggestions; and I feel that I have no right to tell you, "It is nothing," when
everything in your material consciousness is crying out, "Danger!"
   Rest assured that our help and our blessings are always with you.

24 March 1937

Certainly we will be happy to keep you here until June.

You are quite right in saying that these closed doors are an effect of the imagination. The will to pass through always has the power to open them, just as the certainty of victory brightens the path.

12 April 1937

Certainly when you are ready to return, after doing what you want to do for your son, you have only to inform us and we shall be happy to receive you.

Inner calm and peace and an ardent aspiration towards the Divine are the best preparation for receiving the help we can give, and you can be assured of receiving it from us.

29 April 1937

Sudden conversions are usually neither integral nor lasting; they are flashes of lightning which most often dissolve into smoke. Slow and steady effort and persistent striving for progress are more reliable: "piano ma sano".[1]

12 May 1937

Do not let yourself be overwhelmed by the sense of vastness; bathe in it, rather, with joy and serenity. Were we confined inescapably within the four walls of our personal consciousness, that would indeed be sad and overwhelming – but the infinite is open to us; we have only to plunge into it.

29 May 1937

I am sorry that you have been feeling sad these last few days. You should not have. The light should always bring with it the joy of new progress. Now I think that everything will be all right.

10 July 1937

This "Aspiration in the physical" [2] with our blessings and all my love.

Do not let the doctor's words disturb you. Illnesses are never serious unless we accept them as such. Besides, I expect to hear very soon that you are better.

24 July 1938

Here is a little "New Birth".[3]

Indeed, what better use could one make of an illness than to take the opportunity to go deep within oneself and awaken, take birth into a new consciousness, more luminous and more true.

---

[1] Slowly but surely.

[2] The Mother's name for Flame-of-the-woods *(ixora coccinea).*

[3] Sweet Marjoram *(origanum majorana).*

Our help and our blessings are always with you, affectionately.

28 July 1938

Do not worry; you told me long ago – in silence – what you "confessed" to me this evening. And I have always given you the same answer: do not worry; not all gifts need to be material ones – and self-giving is surely the best gift of all.

29 September 1938

These spontaneous reflex actions reveal the subconscious. By tracking down these spontaneous impulses one can gradually clear a path into the virgin forest of the subconscient and bring the Light into it.

Do not worry, and above all do not feel sad! On the 12th the dose was probably a little too strong and, as a result, a little difficult to digest. If you can simply remain quiet, very quiet, everything will settle down. Then the Light will reappear, brighter and more beautiful than ever.

Have no fear – nothing has the power to take you away from me, for I am always with you – in you.

Affectionately.

13 November 1938

Q: Z strongly advises me to take "Genaspirine". I am reluctant, as I never take sedatives. She says it is not a sedative but something to relieve congestion. I understand nothing about it and l told her that I would ask you.

Oh no, no drugs! The more drugs you take, the more you undermine your body's natural resistance.

To relieve tension, ten minutes of real calm, inner and outer, are more effective than all the remedies in the world. In silence lies the most effective help. With our blessings.

30 January 1939

... it is quite clear that if you were in constant contact with the Divine you would be perfectly all right.

Our blessings are always with you.

Very affectionately.

'AIM' May 1996, pages 36-39

Cure of illness by Grace

The Grace is always there ready to act but you must let it work and not resist its action. The one condition required is faith. When you feel attacked, call for help to Sri Aurobindo and myself. If your call is sincere (that is to say, if you sincerely want to be cured) your call will be answered and the Grace will cure you.

Q: When one is caught in an illness, how should one pray to the Mother?

Cure me, O Mother!

... that kind of "miracle" can happen only as the result of an absolute sincerity in the consecration to the Divine and an unshakable faith in the Divine Grace. This was not the case, she was full of fears, desires and demands and terribly concentrated on her exterior being and what she called its needs. This is just the opposite of a sincere consecration.

The chief role of the doctor is, by various means, to induce the body to recover its trust in the Supreme Grace.

I am enclosing a portrait of two birds with *keen eyesight* to encourage you to have faith that your eyes will be cured.

I shall see what can be done.

THE MOTHER

'AIM' April 1988, page 22

* * * * *

Petals of Divine's Love

(Some Answers from the Mother)

Dear Mother,

Lead me to thy own home in Truth... I offer thee my will of progressive submission and increasing adoration.

The way is opened, my dear child, and I am waiting for you with my arms wide to receive and enfold you affectionately.

With my love and blessings.

22 October 1938

Life of my life, I also want to come to you; for, in your arms alone will I have peace and joy and Ananda and the true truth end fulfilment of my life and being. But still... the way is not clear to me. And how shall I be ever able to climb to your dizzying heights with the heavy chains of a mortal's nature pulling at my feet?

Let me carry you in my arms and the climbing will become easy.

Love and blessings to my dear child.

25 October 1938

Dear, dear, dear Mother,

Every day you are growing more and more lovable and more and more adorable to me. By what divine Mystery do you cast this sweet spell on us?

The only mystery, the only spell is my love – my love which is spread over my children and calls down upon them the Divine's Grace to help and to protect.

6 November 1938

Dear Mother, I know your love and blessings are always with me and I sometimes wish you had not been so invariably kind and gracious to me. For it makes it still more hard for me to tell you that there are difficulties of my nature which make it difficult for me to accept you and your Yoga in the requisite spirit. And without this, what is discipleship?

It is not as a Guru that I love and bless, it is as the Mother who asks nothing in return for what she gives.

9 July 1939

Dear, dear, dear Mother,

I send you heaps and heaps of love. In the lotus of my heart may I have your lotus feet permanently installed on a throne of love.

My dear loving child,

Your heart is quite a sweet place because of your love – let me remain always there so that I may fill your whole being with light and love and joy.

My love and blessings.

'AIM' Feb-Mar 1999

Some Questions and Answers

The Mother's Answers:

Q: Sweet Mother, somebody asked me this question: "Is it not a great loss for human society if persons endowed with an exceptional capacity to serve mankind, such as a gifted doctor or barrister, come to stay here in the Ashram for their own salvation? They could perhaps serve the Divine better by serving men and the world!"

Nobody comes here for his own salvation because Sri Aurobindo does not believe in salvation; for us salvation is a meaningless word. We are here to prepare the transformation of the earth and men so that the new creation may take place, and if we make individual efforts to progress, it is because this progress is indispensable for the accomplishment of the work.

I am surprised that after having lived in the Ashram for so long, you can still think in this way and be open to this Sunday-school drivel.

I am sending you a quotation from Sri Aurobindo which will perhaps help to enlighten your thought.

"It is equally ignorant and one thousand miles away from my teaching to find it in your relations with human beings or in the nobility of the human character or an idea that we are here to establish mental and moral and social Truth and justice on human and egoistic lines. I have never promised to do anything of the kind. Human nature is made up of imperfections, even its righteousness and virtue are pretensions, imperfections and prancings of self-approbatory egoism.... What is aimed at by us is a spiritual truth as the basis of life, the first words of which are surrender and union with the Divine and the transcendence of ego. So long as that basis is not established, a sadhak is only an ignorant and imperfect human being struggling with the evils of the lower nature.... What is created by spiritual progress is an inner closeness and intimacy in the inner being, the sense of the Mother's love and presence etc."

Q: Sweet Mother, formerly, You were very strict about permitting people to come and live in the Ashram. Now it is no longer so. Why?

So long as the Ashram was reserved for those who wanted to practise the yoga, it was natural to be strict.

As soon as the children were admitted here, it was no longer possible to be strict and the nature of the life changed.

Now the Ashram has become a symbolic representation of life on earth and everything can find a place in it, provided it has the will to progress towards a diviner life.

Q: Sweet Mother, when a stranger asks us what the Sri Aurobindo Ashram is, how can we give him a reply that is both short and correct?

The Ashram is the cradle of a new world, of the creation of tomorrow.

And if other questions are put to you, the only reply to be made is: you must read the books and study the teaching.

'AIM' June 1999, pages 44 - 45

* * * * *

The Best Object and Idea for Meditation
Words of Sri Aurobindo

Q: What should be the object or ideas for meditation ?

Whatever is most consonant with your nature and highest aspirations. But if you ask me for an absolute answer, then I must say that Brahman is always the best object for meditation or contemplation and the idea on which the mind should fix is that of God in all, all in God and all as God. It does not matter essentially whether it is the Impersonal or the Personal God, or subjectively, the One Self. But this is the idea I have found the best, because it is the highest and embraces all other truths, whether truths of this world or of the other worlds or beyond all phenomenal existence, – "All this is the Brahman."

In the third issue of *Arya*, at the end of the second instalment of the Analysis of the Isha Upanishad, you will find a description of this vision of the All which may be of help to you in understanding the idea.

'AIM' June 1997, page 11

71

A Conversation with the Mother

Mother: Is it January?

Yes, Mother - it is January.

Read what is written here.

"In this year of Sri Aurobindo's centenary, let us strive to be worthy of Him..."

And then?

"...by following His teaching faithfully in order to prepare the advent of the superman. Happy New Year."

What flower is this? *(pointing to the painted flower)*

"Superhumanity".

Eh?

This is "superhumanity". The name of this flower is "superhumanity".

Which flower is it?

This flower - it is the dahlia.

Dahlia! Yes, yes.

(Mother writes the following prayer for the month of February and draws "OM" underneath)

"Nature rediscovers the Divine in a blissful surrender."

With the help of OM one can realise the Divine. OM has a transforming power. OM represents the Divine.

Yes, it represents the Divine. It represents the Divine.

OM, but OM is the sound?

The sound - They say that all the aspirations of the world when going towards the Divine make O---M, like that. *(Mother chants the word)*

'AIM' December 2001
Page 20

* * * * *

European and Indian Music

Q: What is the cause of the great difference between European and Indian music? Is it the origin or the expression ?

It is both but in an inverse sense.

This very high inspiration comes only rarely in European music; rare also is a psychic origin, very rare. Either it comes from high above or it is vital. The expression is almost always, except in a few rare cases, a vital expression – interesting, powerful. Most often, the origin is purely vital. Sometimes it comes

72

from the very heights, then it is wonderful. Sometimes it is psychic, particularly in what has been religious music, but this is not very frequent.

Indian music, when there are good musicians, has almost always a psychic origin; for example, the *rágas* have a psychic origin, they come from the psychic. The inspiration does not often come from above. But Indian music is very rarely embodied in a strong vital. It has rather an inner and intimate origin. I have heard a great deal of Indian music, a great deal; I have rarely heard Indian music having vital strength, very rarely; perhaps not more than four or five times. But very often I have heard Indian music having a psychic origin; it translates itself almost directly into the physical. And truly one must then concentrate, and as it is – how to put it? – very tenuous, very subtle, as there are none of those intense vital vibrations, one can easily glide within it and climb back to the psychic origin of the music. It has that effect upon you, it is a kind of ecstatic trance, as from an intoxication. It makes you enter a little into trance. Then if you listen well and let yourself go, you move on and glide, glide into a psychic consciousness. But if you remain only in the external consciousness, the music is so tenuous that there is no response from the vital, it leaves you altogether flat. Sometimes, there was a vital force, then it became quite good.... I myself like this music very much, this kind of theme developing into a play. The theme is essentially very musical: and then it is developed with variations, innumerable variations, and it is always the same theme which is developed in one way or another. In Europe there were musicians who were truly musicians and they too had the thing: Bach had it, he used to do the same sort of thing. Mozart had it, his music was purely musical, he had no intention of expressing any other thing, it was music for music's sake. But this manner of taking a certain number of notes in a certain relation (they are like almost infinite variations), personally I find it wonderful to put you in repose, and you enter deep within yourself. And then, if you are ready, it gives you the psychic consciousness: something that makes you withdraw from the external consciousness, which makes you enter elsewhere, enter within.

THE MOTHER

'AIM' May 1988, pages 10-11

I caught the echoes of a word supreme

And metred the rhythm-beats of infinity

And listened through music for the eternal Voice.

Sri Aurobindo

(Savitri, p. 405)

The Ascent Towards God

To judge the events of history, a certain distance is needed; similarly, if one knows how to rise high enough above material contingencies, one can see the terrestrial life as a whole. From that moment, it is easy to realise that all the efforts of mankind converge towards the same goal.

It is true that collectively or individually, men follow very different paths to reach it; some of these paths twist and turn so much that they seem at first sight to move away from the goal rather than to lead towards it; but all are going there, consciously or unconsciously, swiftly or more slowly.

What then is this goal?

It is one with the purpose of man's life and his mission in the universe.

The goal: "Call him what you will, for to the wise, he is the Possessor of all names."

The Tao of the Chinese – The Brahman of the Hindus – The Law of the Buddhists – The Good of Hermes – That which cannot be named, according to the ancient Jewish tradition -- The God of the Christians – The Allah of the Muslims – The Justice, the Truth of the materialists.

The purpose of man's life is to become conscious of That.

His mission is to manifest It.

All religions, all the teachings of all the sages are nothing other than methods to reach this goal.

They can be classified into three principal categories.,

First method – intellectual: The love of Truth, the search for the Absolute.

'AIM' Oct 1992, pages 25 - 26

Conversation with a Sadhak*

Words of the Mother

Bonjour!

Bonjour, Sweet Mother.

Something to say?

(I give Her the paper on which is written Thursday 4.5.67)

Oh, it comes on a Thursday! 4.5.67 comes on a Thursday.

Yes, Mother.

It is very well. It comes on a good day. It's good. Then I shall see you on that day, you come to me at three o'clock, do you understand?

(Mother writes on a piece of paper: Mona at three o'clock.)

Otherwise, are you all right? You know, I am not asking you if you are feeling better, or whether everything is all right or not physically, or whether everything is getting along all right or not. All that I know well; actually, I know it better than you do, because I see things you cannot see. All this doesn't interest me; I know all these things very well. I very well know what is happening in you, inwardly as well as outwardly. But I want to know up to which level of consciousness you are conscious and what you can hold. Or to which level of consciousness you have access. What is in question is what you are now doing inwardly, and how far you can open your consciousness to feel the effect. That's what I want to know from you when I ask you how you feel. I want to know what you are conscious of, how far you are able to assimilate the Force and Consciousness I am constantly pouring in. That's what is important for me, and not what happened to you, or if you are feeling uneasy and so on. That's not what I am asking you.

I want to know really in which plane of consciousness you are aware of the work that is going on within you. You can well understand now why each time that I ask you it is to know your state of consciousness and how much progress you are making or to what extent you are conscious of it.

(Silence)

Mother, do the numbers 4.5.67 have an occult significance ?

Occult, yes, but it is quite common. *(A little ironically)* Four, five, six, seven, what is so special about them?

(Silence)

Four, five, six, seven (4.5.67), it is a very rare combination, we don't often come across it. It exercises an extraordinary power over the earth-atmosphere, for example to bring down something. Recently there was a very interesting combination: 6.6.66. Four sixes - this represents the complete square of the Creation. Six is the number which represents Creation. Four sixes – this is very rare. Such a date occurs only once in a century. Lately we had 5.5.55, and as for 7.7.77, when that will come we don't know – it will be at least ... it will be very long before we have this combination.

But 6.6.66 is very important. You know, the old Cabalists said that God created the world in six days, and the sixth day represents Creation – you know the others – and on the seventh day He rested – which is not true, ... for on the seventh day, after completing the Creation He stretched Himself out and lay relaxed in absolute realisation in order to see His work better. It is eternal rest in an immobile and absolute realisation. This is why it has been wrongly thought that the Lord rested, but it was Self-realisation He had undertaken. The Supreme does not rest. It is a wrong notion. In truth, He withdrew into Himself for other realisations, for infinite progress. This will never end. For this He always goes forward to something new. For Him too there is something still to realise. That's how it is ... it goes on.

You see, then, why four sixes are so important, for this makes the square of creation. *(Mother draws a square on the table with Her finger.)* On that day someone was born here – here, I mean someone who lives here with us in the Ashram. I am not speaking of other places – naturally, many were born elsewhere – but for us what is important is that he was born here, in this atmosphere and specially on this date for a conscious development. It is a date chosen by him. Yes, *he* has chosen it. We shall see what he will do. We must follow his development. It is good: he has many possibilities. It is interesting – how these dates which have an occult significance influence physical domains also. We shall see in this child.

Somebody else also had an experience on this day and, besides, it was at 6 in the evening. There is an additional six which makes five sixes – which has a still deeper significance. I don't know where his letter is *(Mother looks for it)* and I don't remember the experience he had exactly. However ...

4.5.67 – what does this signify? Do you know? Manifestation, Power, Creation, Realisation. Four is manifestation, five is power, six, creation and seven, realisation – quite a combination! This is what you must aspire for and what you must realise. You will see what it is. It will be a great day – something will descend ... something ... the beginning ... of the Divine.

Then there is 5.6.78 - no, first there is 7.7.77, but that also - it is very far.

No, Mother, it is only eleven years from now.

But for the combination 4.5.67 we have still to wait for the day ... and 5.6.78 - that too is a very important occasion.

But, Mother, there is still one very important date which

You have left out – 21.2.78.

Oh, yes, that is my centenary....

And 5.6.78 ... this also is an occasion. Above all this, there is the number 8 which represents a double manifestation and a double protection. Well, we shall see what it brings us.

(I give an offering in an envelope. Mother gives me back the empty envelope.)

You can keep it, I don't need it. You can use it to send a letter. Or you can keep it, it will be useful for you.

But shall I take it without anything, Mother?

You want to fill it with something! What do you want, my little one? What can I give you? A blessing?

Mother, something written by You.

(She chooses a card)

Oh, well, this one is beautiful. It is a sheet of paper cut like the leaf of a tree. And it is well done, look. Isn't it? So, I write down the date: 6.6.66 - my Blessings. This date is gone already, but it doesn't matter. You will find out what it means and act accordingly. It will be your duty. To accomplish the square of creation by realising this. It is well, well. I'll see you on Sunday.

Au revoir.

*

Q: This morning after Pranam, Thou blest me with four flowers of Sincerity. I feel that there is special significance in it, but I am unable to find out the same. May I know it?

When I picked up the flowers to give you, I felt that several were coming and I willed: "Let it be the number of the states of the being in which the Sincerity (in the consecration to the Divine) will be definitively established." Four means integrality: the four states of being, mental, psychic, vital, physical.

'AIM' Aug/Sept 1999 pages 11-15

*The conversation which took place on 12 June 1966 is reproduced by the sadhak from memory.

> The Ashram was born a few years after my return from Japan, in 1926.
>
> The Mother
>
> * * *
>
> This Ashram was created with another object than that ordinarily common to such institutions, not for the renunciation of the world but as a centre and a field of practice for the evolution of another kind and form of life which would in the final end be moved by a higher spiritual consciousness and embody a greater life of the spirit.
>
> Sri Aurobindo

On Dates 1.2.'34, 2.3.'45, … 4.5.'67

(Next month we shall have the date 6.7.89 - the numbers occurring consecutively. Last year, in July 1988, we had brought out a special number of All India Magazine on "Significance of Numbers". The following excerpts from the works of Sri Aurobindo and the Mother had not been included in that compilation.)

Q: Sweet Mother, people are saying many things about the 4th of May (1967)[1] – sometimes You too are quoted. But in spite of all this, I have not quite understood its significance.

Is it necessary that it should have a significance?

Sri Aurobindo announced that from that date onwards something would happen.[2] And it did happen.

That is all that is needed.

21 June 1967

[1] The numerical sequence of this date is 4.5.67.

[2] Sri Aurobindo wrote: "1.2.34. It is supposed to be always a year of manifestation, 2.3.45 is the year of power – when the thing manifested gets full force, 4.5.67 is the year of complete realisation." *(From Sri Aurobindo's letter of 2 February 1934)*

*

A conversation that took place on 12 June 1966, recorded from memory

Q: Mother, do the numbers 4.5.67 have an occult significance?

Occult, yes, but it is quite common. *(A little ironically)* Four, five, six, seven, what is so special about them?

(Silence)

Four, five, six, seven (4.5.67), it is a very rare combination, we don't often come across it. It exercises an extraordinary power over the earth-atmosphere, for example to bring down something. Recently there was a very interesting combination: 6.6.66. Four sixes - this represents the complete square of the Creation. Six is the number which represents Creation. Four sixes – this is very rare. Such a date occurs only once in a century. Lately we had 5.5.55, and as for 7.7.77, when that will come we don't know – it will be at least ... it will be very long before we have this combination.

But 6.6.66 is very important. You know, the old Cabalists said that God created the world in six days, and the sixth day represents Creation – you know the others – and on the seventh day He rested – which is not true,... for on the seventh day, after completing the Creation He stretched Himself out and lay relaxed in absolute realisation in order to see His work better. It is eternal rest in an immobile and absolute realisation. This is why it has been wrongly thought that the Lord rested, but it was Self-realisation He had undertaken. The Supreme does not rest. It is a wrong notion. In truth, He withdrew into Himself for other realisations, for infinite progress. This will never end. For this He always goes forward to something new. For Him too there is something still to realise. That's how it is... it goes on.

You see, then, why four sixes are so important, for that makes the square of creation. *(Mother draws a square on the table with Her finger).* On that day someone was born here – here, I mean someone who lives here with us in the Ashram. I am not speaking of other places – naturally, many were born elsewhere – but for us what is important is that he was born here, in this atmosphere and specially on this date for a conscious development. It is a date chosen by him. Yes, he has chosen it. We shall see what he will do. We must follow his development. It is good: he has many possibilities. It is interesting – how these dates which have an occult significance influence physical domains also. We shall see in this child....

4.5.67 – What does this signify? Do you know? Manifestation, Power, Creation, Realisation. Four is manifestation, five is power, six, creation and seven, realisation quite a combination! This is what you must aspire for and what you must realise. You will see what it is. It will be a great day something will descend... something... the beginning... of the Divine.

Champaklal's Notes

Mother had always shown a keen interest in numbers. However busy she might be, certain combinations would not escape her attention.

For instance, when she had to write down the date 24.10.53, she pointed out to me that this date contained all the figures from one to five.

Again on 27.2.72, she remarked that from whichever direction you read, from the left or the right, it is 2,7,2,7,2.

'AIM' June 1989, pages 21 - 23

WORDS OF THE MOTHER:

Significance of Birthdays*

It is your birthday tomorrow?

Sadhak: Yes, Mother.

How old will you be?

Sadhak: Twenty-six, Mother.

I shall see you tomorrow and give you something special. You will see, I am not speaking of anything material that, I shall give you a card and all that – but of something... You will see, tomorrow, now go home and prepare yourself quietly so that you may be ready to receive it.

Sadhak: Yes, Mother.

You know, my child, what "Bonne Fête" signifies, that is, the birthday we wish here?...

Sadhak: Like that, I know what it means, Mother, but not the special significance You want to tell me.

Yes, it is truly a special day in one's life. It is one of those days in the year when the Supreme descends into us - or when we are face to face with the Eternal – one of those days when our soul comes in contact with the Eternal and, if we remain a little conscious, we can feel His Presence within us. If we make a little effort on this day, we accomplish the work of many lives as in a lightning flash. That is why I give so much importance to the birthday – because what one gains in one day is truly something incomparable. And it is for this that I also work to open the consciousness a little towards what is above so that one may come before the Eternal. My child, it is a very very special day, for it is the day of decision, the day one can unite with the Supreme Consciousness. For the Lord lifts us on this day to the highest region possible so that our soul which is a portion of that Eternal Flame, may be united and identified with its Origin.

This day is truly an opportunity in life. One is so open and so receptive that one can assimilate all that is given. I can do many things, that is why it is important.

*A spoken comment of the Mother which was noted down from memory by the sadhak and later read to the Mother

It is one of those days when the Lord Himself opens the doors wide for us. It is as though He were inviting us to rekindle more powerfully the flame of aspiration. It is one of those days which He gives us. We too, by our personal effort, could attain to this, but it would be long, hard and not so easy. And this – this is a real chance in life – the day of the Grace.

It is an occult phenomenon that occurs invariably, without our knowledge, on this particular day of the year. The soul leaves behind the body and journeys up and up till it merges into the Source in order to replenish itself and absorb from the Supreme Its Power, Light and Ananda and comes down charged for a whole year to pass. Then again and again... it continues like this year after year.

*

A Birthday Message and Prayer
Given by the Mother to a Sadhak

A grain of practice is worth a mountain of theories.

"Lord, on this anniversary day of my birth, grant that the power to know changes in me into a power to transform myself integrally."

'AIM' June, pages 4 - 5

The 24th November is called the day of Victory in remembrance of a very important spiritual event which took place in 1926.

The Mother

* * *

It was the descent of Krishna into the physical.

Sri Aurobobindo

* * *

Krishna is the supramental Light. The descent of Krishna would mean the descent of the Overmind Godhead preparing, though not itself actually, the descent of Supermind and Ananda. Krishna is the Anandamaya; he supports the evolution through the Overmind leading it towards the Ananda.

Sri Aurobindo

THE FORCE OF BODY-CONSCIOUSNESS

THERE is a state of consciousness in which you perceive that the effect of things, circumstances, movements, all the activities of life upon yourself depends almost exclusively upon your attitude towards them. You become then conscious, conscious to the extent of realising that things in themselves are neither good nor bad, they are so only in relation to ourselves: their effect, I say, depends entirely upon the way in which we regard these things.

If we take, for example, a circumstance as a gift from God, as a divine Grace, as an outcome of the total harmony, it will help us to become more conscious and truer and stronger. The same identical circumstance, if we take it differently, as a blow of Fate, as a bad force wishing us harm, becomes, on the contrary, a, damper on our consciousness, it saps our strength, brings obscurity, creates disharmony. And yet in either case it is altogether the same circumstance. I would like you to have the experience and make the experiment. For your ideal is to be master of yourselves. But not that only. You should not only be master of your own selves, but master of the circumstances of your life, the circumstances, at least, that immediately surround you and concern you. You must note further that it is an experience that is not confined to the mind alone: it need not happen in your head only, it may and indeed must continue into the body.

Certainly, this is a realisation needing great labour, much concentration and self-mastery: you have to force the consciousness into the body, into dense Matter. It is the attitude of the body that will in the end determine everything: shocks and contacts of the outside world will change its nature according to the way in which they are received by the body. And if you attain perfection in that line, you can become even master of accidents. Such a thing is possible, not only possible, but it is bound to happen, for it is a forward step in man's progress. First of all, you have to realise the power in your mind to the extent that it can act upon circumstances and change their effect upon you. Then the power can descend into Matter, into the substance, the cells of your body and endow the body with this capacity of control over things outside and around you.

There is nothing impossible in the world. We ourselves put the bar: always we say, this is possible, that is impossible, one can do this, one cannot do that. Sometimes we admit a thing to be possible but ask who would do it, so it is impossible and so on. Like slaves, like prisoners we bind ourselves to our limits. You call it common sense, but it is a stupid, narrow and ignorant sense; it does not truly know the laws of life. The laws of life are not what we think them to be, what our mind or intellect conceives them to be; they are quite otherwise.

EARTH A SYMBOL

THE earth is the centre of the material universe. It has been created for concentrating the force that is to transform Matter. It is the symbol of the divine potentiality in Matter. As we have said, the earth was created through a direct intervention of the Divine Consciousness: it is on the earth alone that there is and can be the direct contact with the Divine. The earth absorbs and develops and radiates the divine light; its radiation spreads through space and extends wherever there is Matter. The material universe shares, to some extent, the gift that the earth brings – the light and harmony of the Divine Consciousness. But it is upon the Earth alone that there is the full and flnal flowering of that consciousness.

NOLINI KANTA GUPTA

(Based on a talk by The Mother)

'SRI AUROBINDO ACTION' January 1975

We all who have a common uplifting ideal, shall unite; and in this union and by this union we will face and overcome the attacks of all opposing forces of darkness and devastation. In union is the strength, in union is the power, in union the certitude of Victory.

The Mother

1973 Conversations with the Teachers

(The six conversations held with one or two teachers of the Sri Aurobindo International Centre of Education, Sri Aurobindo Ashram, in 1973, are the last recorded statements of the Mother on the subject of education.)

8 February 1973

A: What is the best way of preparing ourselves, until we can establish a new system?

Naturally, it is to widen and illumine your consciousness – but how to do it? Your own consciousness... to widen and illumine it. And if you could find, each one of you, your psychic and unite with it, all the problems would be solved.

The psychic being is the representative of the Divine in the human being. That's it, you see – the Divine is not something remote and inaccessible. The Divine is in you but you are not fully conscious of it. Rather you have... it acts now as an influence rather than as a Presence. It should be a conscious Presence, you should be able at each moment to ask yourself what is... how... how the Divine sees. It is like that: first how the Divine sees, and then how the Divine wills and then how the Divine acts. And it is not to go away into inaccessible regions, it is right here. Only, for the moment, all the old habits and the general unconsciousness put a kind of covering which prevents us from seeing and feeling. You must... you must lift, you must lift that up.

In fact, you must become conscious instruments... conscious... conscious of the Divine.

Usually this takes a whole lifetime, or sometimes, for some people it is several lifetimes. Here, in the present conditions, you can do it in a few months. For those who are... who have an ardent aspiration, in a few months they can do it.

(Long silence)

Did you feel anything?

Be completely sincere. Say whether you felt anything, or whether there was no difference for you. Completely sincere. Well? Nobody is answering. *(Mother asks each person in turn and each gives his or her reaction.)*

B: Sweet Mother, may I ask you whether there was a special descent?

There is no descent. That is another wrong idea: there is no descent. It is something that is always there but which you do not feel. There is no descent: it is a completely wrong idea.

Do you know what the fourth dimension is? Do you know what it is?

B: We have heard about it....

Do you have the experience?

B: No, Sweet Mother.

Ah! But in fact that is the best approach of modern science: the fourth dimension. The Divine, for us, is the fourth dimension... within the fourth dimension. It is everywhere, you see, everywhere, always. It does not come and go, it is there, always, everywhere. It is we, our stupidity which prevents us from feeling. There is no need to go away, not at all, not at all, not at all.

To be conscious of your psychic being, you must once be capable of feeling the fourth dimension, otherwise you cannot know what it is.

My God! For seventy years I have known what the fourth dimension is... more than seventy years!

(Silence)

Indispensable, indispensable! Life begins with that. Otherwise one is in falsehood, in a muddle and in confusion and in darkness. The mind, mind, mind, mind! Otherwise, to be conscious of your own consciousness, you have to mentalise it. It is dreadful, dreadful!

A: The new life, Mother, is not the continuation of the old, is it? It springs up from within.

Yes, yes...

A: There is nothing in common between...

There is, there is, but you are not conscious of it. But you must, you must... It is the mind which prevents you from feeling it. You must be... You mentalise everything, everything... What you call consciousness is the thinking of things, that is what you call consciousness: the thinking of things. But it is not that at all, that is not consciousness. The consciousness must be capable of being totally lucid and without words.

(Silence)

There, everything becomes luminous and warm... strong! And peace, the true peace, which is not inertia and which is not immobility.

A: And Mother, can this be given as an aim to all the children?

All... no. They are not all of the same age, even when they are of the same age physically. There are children who... who are at an elementary stage. You should... If you were fully conscious of your psychic, you would know the children who have a developed psychic. There are children in whom the psychic is only embryonic. The age of the psychic is not the same, far from it. Normally the psychic takes several lives to form itself completely, and it is that which passes from one body to another and that is why we are not conscious of our past lives: it is because we are not conscious of our psychic. But sometimes, there is a moment when the psychic has participated in an event; it has become conscious, and that makes a memory. One sometimes has... one sometimes has a fragmentary recollection, the memory of a circumstance or an event, or of a thought or even an act, like that: this is because the psychic was conscious.

You see how it is, now I am nearing a hundred, it's only five years away now. I started making an effort to become conscious at five years old, my child. This is to let you know.... And I go on, and it goes on. Only... Of course, I have come to the point where I am doing the work for the cells of the body, but still, the work began a long time ago.

This is not to discourage you, but... it is to let you know that it does not happen just like that!

The body... the body is made of a substance which is still very heavy, and it is the substance itself which has to change for the Supermind to be able to manifest.

There you are.

'AIM' Nov 1994, pages 16 - 19

About the Photograph on the Facing Page:

(Mona Sarkar asks the Mother:)

Mother, why are You doing pranam in this photograph? Why? And to whom?

(Mother's Reply recollected from memory:)

Don't you see that I am greeting the Truth? This is the necessary posture. It is the attitude of adoration and humility, I wait patiently for the day when Truth will be the sole guide. And it is so important, this attitude. If the earth wants the Divine Truth to be established here, in its entirety, this is the attitude it must take. This is the only thing which can save the earth.

To remain in this attitude and aspire upwards. The earth must learn to bow before the Truth with this attitude. This is adoration as well as obeisance. This is what it must learn; it represents much more, it is something profound and sublime.

'AIM' June 1994, pages 16 - 17

If you follow your mind, it will not recognise the Mother even when she is manifest before you. Follow your soul and not your mind, your soul that answers to the Truth, not your mind that leaps at appearances. Trust the Divine Power and she will free the godlike elements in you and shape all into an expression of Divine Nature.

Sri Aurobindo

THE MOTHER
Adoration and Obeisance

SECTION IV

Words of the Mother

There is an ascending evolution in nature which goes from the stone to the plant, from the plant to the animal, from the animal to man. Because man is, for the moment, the last rung at the summit of the ascending evolution, he considers himself as the final stage in this ascension and believes there can be nothing on earth superior to him. In that he is mistaken. In his physical nature he is yet almost wholly an animal, a thinking and speaking animal, but still an animal in his material habits and instincts. Undoubtedly, nature cannot be satisfied with such an imperfect result; she endeavours to bring out a being who will be to man what man is to the animal, a being who will remain a man in its external form, and yet whose consciousness will rise far above the mental and its slavery to ignorance.

Sri Aurobindo came upon earth to teach this truth to men. He told them that man is only a transitional being living in a mental consciousness, but with the possibility of acquiring a new consciousness, the Truth-consciousness, and capable of living a life perfectly harmonious, good and beautiful, happy and fully conscious.

The Mother
CWM Vol. 12, p. 116

Sri Aurobindo said that the divine life will manifest on earth, because it is *already* involved in the depths of Matter....

The children should be told: There are wonderful things to be manifested, prepare yourself to receive them. Then if they want something a little more concrete and easier to understand, you can tell them: Sri Aurobindo came to announce these things; when you are able to read him, you will understand.

The Mother
CWM Vol. 12, pp. 404-05

There is no end to the wonders of the Universe. The more we get free from the limits of our small ego, the more these wonders disclose themselves to us.

The Mother

Is Sri Aurobindo's Teaching a New Religion?
Words of the Mother

Q: Many people say that the teaching of Sri Aurobindo is a new religion. Would you say that it is a religion?

People who say that are fools who don't even know what they are talking about. You only have to read all that Sri Aurobindo has written to know that it is impossible to base religion on his works, because he presents each problem, each question in all its aspects, showing the truth contained in each way of seeing things, and he explains that in order to attain the Truth you must realise a synthesis which goes beyond all mental notions and emerge into a transcendence beyond thought.
...when we speak of Sri Aurobindo there can be question of a teaching nor even of a revelation, but of an action from the Supreme; no religion can be founded on that.

But men are so foolish that they can change anything into a religion, so great is their need of a fixed framework for their narrow thought and limited action. They do not feel secure unless they can assert this is true and that is not; but such an assertion becomes impossible for anyone who has read and understood what Sri Aurobindo has written. Religion and Yoga do not belong to the same plane of being and spiritual life can exist in all its purity only when it is free from all mental dogma.

*

Till the birth of Sri Aurobindo, religions and spiritualities were always centred on past figures, and they were showing as 'the goal' the negation of life upon earth. So, you had a choice between two alternatives: either – a life in this world with its round of petty pleasures and pains, joys and sufferings, threatened by hell if you were not behaving properly, or – an escape into another world, heaven, nirvana, moksha...

Between these two there is nothing much to choose, they are equally bad.

Sri Aurobindo has told us that this was a fundamental mistake, which accounts for the weakness and degradation of India. Buddhism, Jainism, Illusionism were sufficient to sap all energy out of the country.

True, India is the only place in the world, which is still aware that something else than Matter exists...

Sri Aurobindo has shown that the truth does not lie in running away from earthly life but in remaining in it, to transform it, divinise it, so that the Divine can manifest HERE, in this PHYSICAL WORLD.

*

[Sri Aurobindo on Himself]
It is not his object to develop any one religion or to amalgamate the older religions or to found any new religion – for any of these things would lead away from his central purpose. The one aim of his Yoga is an inner self-development by which each one who follows it in time discover the One Self in all and evolve a higher consciousness than the mental, – a spiritual and supramental consciousness which will transform and divinise human nature.

AIM Nov. 2001 page 46-47

Wars and Destructions
Words of Sri Aurobindo

Man is a quarrelling and fighting animal and so long as he is so how can there be peace?

*

Our work is not to fight these things but to bring down a higher nature and a Truth-creation which will make spiritual Light and Power the chief force in terrestrial existence.

*

Destruction in itself is neither good nor evil. It is a fact of Nature, a necessity in the play of forces, as things are in this world. The light destroys the Darkness and the Powers of Darkness, and that is not a movement of Ignorance!

It all depends on the character of the destruction and the forces that enter into it. All dread of fire or other violent forces should be overcome. For dread shows a weakness – the free spirit can stand fearless before even the biggest forces of Nature.

*

I have also supported justifiable violence on justifiable occasions, e.g., Kurukshetra and the war against Hitler and all he means. The question then, from this middle point of view, about the immediate question is whether this violence is justifiable and the occasion justifiable. I back out.

(SABCL. 22: 490-92)

The Foundation of the Future

The time of religions is over.

We have entered the age of universal spirituality, of spiritual experience in its initial purity.

The Mother

The Truth of the Divine which is the spiritual reality behind all religions and the descent of the supramental which is not known to any religion are the sole things which will be the foundation of the work in the future.

Sri Aurobindo
(Source: CWM 15:32. SA Circle 1976: i)

A Divinely Chosen Country

India has become the symbolic representation of all the difficulties of modern mankind.

India will be the land of its resurrection – the resurrection to a higher and truer life.

*

In the whole creation the earth has a place of distinction, because unlike any other planet it is evolutionary with a psychic entity at its centre. In it, India, in particular, is a divinely chosen country.

*

From time immemorial (some scholars say 8000 years BC before the Christian era) India has been the land of spiritual knowledge and practice, of the discovery of the Supreme Reality and union with it. It is the country that has practised concentration most and best. The methods, called Yoga in Sanskrit, that are taught and used in this country are countless. Some are merely material, others purely intellectual, others religious and devotional; lastly, some of them combine these various processes in order to achieve a more integral result.

*

From the spiritual point of view, India is the foremost country in the world. Her mission is to set the example of spirituality. Sri Aurobindo came on earth to teach this to the world.

AIM April 1996 page 35

Do not forget even for a moment that has been created by Him out of Himself. Not only is He present in everything, but also He is everything. The differences are only in expression and manifestation. If you forget this you lose everything.

*

I would say, may the world become aware that the Divine is manifesting.

The Mother

The Great Adventure

In the supramental creation there will no longer be any religions. The whole life will be the expression, the flowering into forms of the divine unity manifesting in the world. And there will no longer be what individuals now call gods.

These great divine beings themselves will be able to participate in the new creation, but to do so, they will have to put on what we could call the "Supramental substance" on earth. And if some of them choose to remain in their world as they are, if they decide not to manifest physically, their relation with the beings of supramental earth will be a relation of friend, collaborators, equals, for the highest divine essence will be manifestation in the beings of the new supramental world on earth. When the physical substance is supramentalised, to incarnate on earth will no longer be a cause of inferiority, quite the contrary. It will give a plenitude which cannot be obtained otherwise.

But all this is in the future; it is a future ...... which has begun, but will take some time to be realised integrally. Meanwhile we are in a very special situation, extremely special, without precedent. We are now witnessing the birth of a new world; it is very young, very weak – not in its essence but in its outer manifestation – not yet recognised, not even felt, denied by the majority.

But it is here. It is here making an effort to grow, absolutely sure of the result. But the road to it is a completely new road which has never before been traced out- nobody had gone there, nobody has done that! It is a beginning, a universal beginning. So it is an absolutely unexpected and unpredictable adventure.

There are people who love adventure. It is there I call, and I tell them this:- "I invite you to the great adventure."

It is not a question of repeating spiritually what others have done before us, for our adventure begins beyond that. It is a question of a new creation, entirely new, with all the unforeseen events, the risk, the hazards it entails – a real adventure, whose goal is certain victory, but the road to which is unknown and must be traced out step by step in the unexplored. Something that has never been in the present universe and that will never be again in the same way. If that interests you. well, let us embark. What will happen to you tomorrow – I have no idea.

One must put aside all that has been foreseen, all that has been advised, all that has been constructed, and then ...... set off walking into the unknown. And – come what may! There.

10 July 1957   The Mother

" Sri Aurobindo's Action" April 2000

An Interview with William Greaves

Tell us how you discovered Pondicherry.

It's an interesting story. It happened way back in 1950, in Harlem. I was attending some lectures on ancient African history and there happened to be two Indian students in the study group. One was Balkrishna Shelar and the other one was named Ram. I can't recall his last name. After class, the three of us would get together and have these stimulating discussions, and often we would end up in the basement of the new Indian consulate where they were lodged. They would make curry and we would continue our discussions and even the occasional argument. One day we were arguing about the meaning of art. I started talking about André Malraux, and finally Ram said to me: "Bill, you don't know anything about art!" You shotuld read *The National Value of Art* by Sri Aurobindo. "It's a wonderful book", he said, "I'll get you a copy."

So he gave me a copy of *The National Value of Art*. I read it and it blew my mind! I was quite overwhelmed by it. I had never come across anything so profound, so insightful, so inspiring!

Did you ever meet the Mother?

No, no, I never did. Curiously, I didn't even know the Mother existed till the mid 1960s. Even reading through the books, whenever there were any references made to the Mother I always imputed it to a Cosmic Principle. I didn't even know of Her till 1965 or so when I met Chitra Neogy. I was at a function at the Indian consulate. I saw Sri Aurobindo's symbol on a necklace Chitra was wearing and I said: "Where are you from?" She said from India. I said, "You've got this symbol of Sri Aurobindo." She said "Yes, I wear it often." Then she began talking about the Mother, she would say "the Mother this and the Mother that." I said: "Who is this Mother?" Then Chitra told me. That's how I became aware of the Mother, this powerful presence in the Ashram and in Auroville that everyone speaks about.

And when was the first time you came to Pondicherry?

I think it was somewhere around 1979. I was a member of the Indo-US Sub-commission on Education and Culture. I was on the media committee. We were trying, as members of the committee, to expand cultural relations between India and the United States. So, in a sense, that was my ticket to India. Once I got to India I headed for Pondicherry, for Sri Aurobindo. Actually, I was in India before then, in 1963, making a film for the United Nations. But I wasn't able to visit Pondicherry at the time.

Courtesy: "The Golden Chain" Aug 2001,
the Alumni Journal of Sri Aurobindo International Centre of Education

The Lost Footsteps

...Then two days before the moment which I was awaiting so feverishly, the whole team of warders was replaced by a new one and I had to give up my plan. I was overwhelmed by frustration, I felt as if I had been crushed by an avalanche and buried under the debris so that I could scarcely breathe.

After this my hallucinations became very frequent.

One evening, when the radiator had begun its mournful music, the wall in front of me rolled back and a chain of snowy mountains gleamed in the rising sun. In the foreground was a little Indian temple dedicated to the goddess Kali. A tall tree shaded it. At its foot an old man sat with his legs tucked under him and his hands resting on his knees in Brahmin fashion. He had a long and very thin white beard. His ascetic face had the same serenity as the blue sky stretching over the dazzling peaks. As I gazed at him he bowed his head slightly, smiled and said: "I can see you have forgotten me. Don't you remember Aurobin Dogos*, the Brahmin?"

I heard myself replying: "You have no idea how long I have been looking for you and calling you . . ."

"I had to make a long journey to get here," he said. "It took me sixty years."

For months after this I lived in the company of the "Brahmin" whom I believed at the time to be a real person other than myself. But these visions were different in character from the nightmare hallucinations I had had before. It seemed that, somehow, I had reached a deeper level of my being and these new experiences, instead of helping my enemies, marked the beginning of a period of spiritual integration.

I held long conversations with the "hermit" and it was "he" who argued me out of committing suicide, persuading me that life was sacred and must be lived to the last breath.

I complained to him that, locked inside these walls and thinking ceaselessly night and day without a moment's respite, I had reached the limits of my endurance. "Tell me," I begged him, "am I the victim of these men who hold me captive, or at the mercy of some harsh, blind laws of nature?"

He explained to me his view of suffering. "Some people it destroys," he said, "others are challenged by it to resist some evil or to undertake some positive, creative act; some are corrupted, lose control over themselves and become cruel and vengeful, others grow in strength and grace."

"But what can a man do alone, armed with nothing but his free will, against an overwhelming evil?" I asked him.

In answer, he told me a story.

Two swallows nested under the eaves of a fisherman's hut near the sea-shore. Teaching their young to fly, they took them out over the sea, gradually training them to cross long distances and to face the hardships they would have to undergo during their migration. The fledgelings shot into the air, exulting in the joy of flight and freedom, but a gust of wind caught one of them and flung it down upon the surface of the waves. The small bird kept its wings outstretched so that it did not sink, but neither could it rise; floating like a leaf, it called piteously to its parents as they circled over it. The parent swallows did their best to calm and to encourage it, then they flew back to the shore and made innumerable journeys to the water's edge, each time carrying a

*Aurobindo Ghose is the real name corrected by the compiler.

drop of water in their beaks and pouring it into the sand. Thus they hoped to empty the ocean and to save their young.

"Their heroic effort is a lesson to us," the "Brahmin" went on. "The human will and spirit must also not be resigned at moments of crisis; it must go on looking for a solution, however overwhelming the odds. You must not accept defeat, you must not believe your efforts to be in vain. If you have the blind courage to continue to endure and to struggle, you will find a new beginning in your life."

My conversations with the hermit living in solitude near the temple to the goddess Kali had lasted several months. Outside spring was appearing; the strength of the light and a suspicion of warmth in the air were the first signs. Who was the "Brahmin"? Why was he trying to give me precious support? Understanding my perplexity, he gently held out a pale, skeleton-like hand and stroked my forehead with his cold fingers. Somehow transfigured, he said to me with emotion:

"You want to know who I am? I am your spirit; your reason! You appealed to me in a moment of abject despair. In your isolation and helplessness, only I am capable of encouraging you to bolster your morale and strengthen your will; apart from me, there is no one who is able to come to your aid. Put your trust in my strength and you will never regret it!"

This encounter was indeed a turning point in my existence. Gradually my nightmares left me and I discovered an inner calm and balance and achieved control over my mind and body.

After days and weeks of practice I found that I could sit motionless on my chair for hours, my head leaning gently against the wall and my eyes open. I breathed deeply and quietly, my will controlling my heart-beats and keeping them steady. Hunger and fatigue took less toll of my strength than when I had dissipated it in pacing up and down my cell, fighting against drowsiness. My small ration of food and the two or three hours' sleep I was allowed out of the twenty-four were now sufficient for my bodily needs.

To detach my mind totally from my surroundings took more time and effort. At first I told myself that I was a spectator in a darkened room: my prison life was nothing but a film projected on a screen, which I trained myself to interrupt at will. At a later stage I succeeded in looking upon my body, sitting motionless in the chair, as though it were a photograph. Still later I felt my spirit able to escape the prison walls and undertake long journeys.

The warders were puzzled by the transformation which had taken place before their eyes: a man who had been frantic, driven to the verge of madness by lack of sleep, now sat calm and as still as a statue. From time to time they knocked on the door and ordered me to move my head or blink my eyes, to make sure that I was still alive and lucid. Inwardly I had reached a peace and a serenity which I had never known before.

Time no longer dragged; solitude was not a hardship, it was the opportunity for ceaseless contemplation. Freed from its anxieties, my mind devoted itself passionately to pure thought. I now longed to survive – even, if need be, in prison – for I was enchanted by the happiness of my new spiritual freedom. I longed to encompass the universe, to search its mysteries, as inexhaustible as infinity.

"The Lost Footsteps", p-p 166-169
© Silvu Craciuna 1961

Mother on The Ashram

None of the present achievements of humanity, however great they are, can be for us an ideal to follow. The wide world is there as a field of experiment for human ideals.

Our purpose is quite different and if our chances of success are small just now, we are sure that we are working to prepare the future.

I know that from the external point of view we are below many of the present achievements in this world, but our aim is not a perfection in accordance with the human standards. We are endeavouring for something else which belongs to the future.

The Ashram has been founded and is meant to be the cradle of the new world.

The inspiration is from above, the guiding force is from above, the creative power is from above, at work for the descent of the new realisation.

It is only by its shortcomings, its deficiencies and its failures that the Ashram belongs to the present world.

None of the present achievements of humanity have the power to pull the Ashram out of its difficulties.

It is only a total conversion of all its members and an integral opening to the descending Light of Truth that can help it to realise itself.

The task, no doubt, is a formidable one, but we received the command to accomplish it and we are upon earth for that purpose alone.

We shall continue up to the end with an unfailing trust in the Will and the Help of the Supreme.

The door is open and will always remain open to all those who decide to give their life for that purpose.

The Mother
13 June 1964
Collected Works Vol.13 p.113.

Redeeming Ganges

Churches, Orders, theologies, philosophies have failed to save mankind because they have busied themselves with intellectual creeds, dogmas, rites and institutions, with ācāraśuddhi and darśana, as if these could save mankind, and have neglected the one thing needful, the power and purification of the soul. We must go back to the one thing needful, take up again Christ's gospel of the purity and perfection of mankind, Mahomed's gospel of perfect submission, self-surrender and servitude of God, Chaitanya's gospel of the perfect love and joy of God in man, Ramakrishna's gospel of the unity of all religions and the divinity of God in man, and, gathering all these streams into one mighty river, one purifying and redeeming Ganges, pour it over the death-in-life of a materialistic humanity as Bhagiratha led down the Ganges and flooded with it the ashes of his fathers, so that there may be a resurrection of the soul in mankind and the Satyayuga for a while return to the world.

(SABCL Vol. 16, p. 430)   **Sri Aurobindo**

DID YOU KNOW

The Dawn and Dawn Society's Magazine had reported the National Education Conference held at Pabna, East Bengal, on 13th February 1908, in its April 1908 issue as under:

"Srijukta Aurobindo Ghose... pointed out that the University system was defective in its aims and methods intended only to serve the purposes of the Government, not the requirements of the country. It turned out machines for administrative and professional work, not men. The national system of education was intended to create a nation. It must produce men with all their faculties trained, full of patriotism, and mentally, morally, physically the equals of the men of any other nation."

(Source: *Speeches,* Sri Aurobindo Ashram, 1974 ed., p. 46)

*

It was February, 1835. A time when the British were striving to take control of the whole of India. Lord Macaulay, a historian and a politician, made a historical speech in the British Parliament, commonly referred to as The Minute, which struck a blow at the centuries fresh tree of Indian education. His words were to this effect:

I have travelled across the length and breadth of India and I have not seen one person who is a beggar, who is a thief. Such wealth I have seen in this country, such high moral values, people of such caliber, that I do not think we would ever conquer this country, unless we break the very backbone of this nation, which is her spiritual and cultural heritage, and therefore I propose that we replace her old and ancient education system, her culture, for if the Indians think that all that is foreign and English is good and greater than their own, they will lose their self-esteem, their native self-culture and they will become what we want them, a truly dominated nation.

(Source: *The Awakening Ray,* Vol. 4, No. 5, The Gnostic Centre)

AIM June 2001

*

Q: Are there really any beings on Jupiter or Mars?

For me, if you ask me, there are beings everywhere. Everywhere. One doesn't see them, that's all. But they are everywhere. But certainly I don't think they are like what we see in the pictures – the Martians you were shown in the pictures with grotesque forms. I have no reason to think that they are like that.

The Mother
'AIM' July 2002

"WHO IS SRI AUROBINDO?"

ONCE in the early years of my life in the Ashram I wrote to Sri Aurobindo, "How people calling to Shiva or Krishna or their Ishta Devata get responses from you I don't understand." He replied, "Who is Shiva? and also who is Krishna? and what is an Ishta Devata? There is only one Divine, not a thousand Divines." Myself: "It would mean that wherever a sincere heart is aspiring for the Divine, his aspiration reaches your ears." Sri Aurobindo: "Why my ears? Ears are not necessary for the purpose. You might as well say, reaches me by the post." I then protested, "No, Sir, I am satisfied with you as Sri Aurobindo pure and simple. I don't need anybody else." He wrote back, "No objection. I only suggested that I don't know who this Sri Aurobindo pure and simple is. If you do, I congratulate you." Since then, my relation with him had become very intimate. I gradually came to know many aspects of his personality, but never who he really was. My correspondence with him has shown that I dared to take liberties with him (which was considered unthinkable by other sadhaks). Once I wrote to him: "Cut me or beat me, Sir, but don't forsake me." And the answer he wrote back startled me and filled me with a sudden delight and assurance beyond measure. He wrote, "Never. But beat you, a lot." This assurance has sustained and will sustain me even in my future life, if I may say so. Once I dared to ask him, "Where do you get so much sense of humour?" His cryptic reply: ""fl" < fl: (*raso vai sah* – verily He is Delight.) Then one day when I asked him: "Why are you so soft and free as if I'm your comrade?" He gave an enigmatic answer: "Find out for yourself." When I failed to find out, he wrote: "It is not by the mind that you can find out." Till now I have failed to discover why. The enigma remains unsolved and I live with the hope that perhaps he will divulge the secret as he has divulged to Dilip the cause of his intimacy with him. But he has made me stick to him till now and perhaps forever.

But my knowledge of him has grown as far as my small human understanding can allow. And I have come to this conclusion that what he has written about Sri Krishna in fact applies to him too. In his estimation Sri Krishna had an unfathomable mind of knowledge. Sri Aurobindo remains an enigma to the world. The Mother herself has admitted that she had failed to know him though she had lived with him for more than 30 years. To a disciple who wished to write his biography, he remarked that his life has not been on the surface for people to see.

The vast world of knowledge he possessed remains unparalleled. He has himself admitted to us that what he knows will remain untold even if he goes on writing for twelve years. We asked him, "Will all that knowledge remain unknown to us and posterity?" "Learn first of all what I have written," he replied with a sweet smile, and added, "I am afraid I have come perhaps before my time." Comes to mind a mighty line from one of his poems: "I have drunk the Infinite like a giant's wine." Only with the help of such a Wine could he have given to India and the world his four major contributions: a national awakening and fiery thirst for total independence, a new and deeper interpretation of the Vedas, the rediscovery of the Supermind, and a life-embracing system of Integral Yoga.

The question that makes us marvel with wonder is how within a short span of years he could gather so vast a knowledge, and even record it, which would need at least a hundred years. The Mother holds an answer to that enigma. She said that he had only to sit before the typewriter and knowledge would pour down like a stream from above.

And is it only knowledge? What about the beauty of expression, perfection of style and masterly composition? We remember that when his immortal book The Life Divine had been published, The Times Literary Supplement's front page article described Sri Aurobindo as "an author who writes with the sky for page and the constellations as his company," and as "a new kind of thinker who combines the serenity of the East and the alacrity of the West". Romain Rolland, a great French savant, said about Sri Aurobindo, "The old leader of the Bengal revolt, who is now one of the greatest thinkers of modern India, has realised the most complete synthesis achieved up to the present between the genius of the West and that of the East". He also said that Sri Aurobindo is the last of the great Rishis who holds the creative bow in his hand.

If this is about the man of Knowledge, what about the human being he was?. What has he got not done for the human race? We know he sacrificed his inestimable life for the incalculable benefit of man. In the Mother's revelation to Dr. Sanyal a famous surgeon who was called to treat Sri Aurobindo: "People do not know what a tremendous sacrifice he has made for the world. About a year ago, while I was discussing things I remarked that I felt like leaving the body. He spoke out in a firm tone, 'No this can never be. If necessary for the transformation I might go, you will have to fulfil our yoga of supramental descent and transformation'," She also said: "As soon as Sri Aurobindo withdrew form his body, what he called the Mind of Light got realised in me". And his human body as we would say turned a golden colour for five days to the surprise of the public. But his immortal consciousness is ever with us guiding the destiny of the world, remaining with us in all our trials and tribulation and leading this woe-begotten race to its divine destiny for which he came to the world – a colonist from Immortality!

What shall we then think of him? That he is as God himself is? Have we got the answer to his question "Who is Sri Aurobindo?" Or will he remain a marvellous enigma forever?

"Mother India" Sept. 1999, pages 907-908

A Message From The Mother

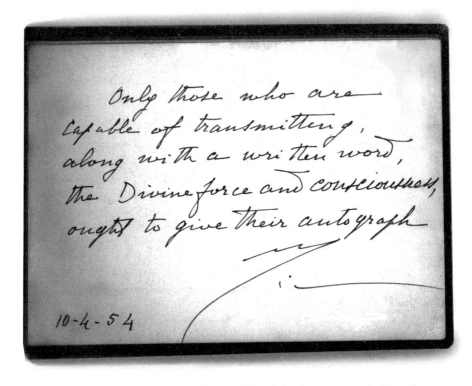

Given to Bhanabhai Patel in his Autograph Book

'Only those who are capable of transmitting, along with a written word, the Divine force and consciousness, ought to give their autograph'